HANDBOOK OF PSYCHIATRIC PRACTICE IN THE JUVENILE COURT

The Workgroup on Psychiatric Practice in the Juvenile Court
of the American Psychiatric Association

Michael G. Kalogerakis, M.D., Chair

Published by the
American Psychiatric Association
1400 K Street, N.W.
Washington, DC 20005

Note: The contributors have worked to ensure that all information in this book concerning drug dosages, schedules, and routes of administration is accurate as of the time of publication and consistent with standards set by the U.S. Food and Drug Administration and the general medical community. As medical research and practice advance, however, therapeutic standards may change. For this reason and because human and mechanical errors sometimes occur, we recommend that readers follow the advice of a physician who is directly involved in their care or the care of a member of their family.

The findings, opinions, and conclusions of this report do not necessarily represent the views of officers, trustees, or all members of the American Psychiatric Association. This report represents the judgment and consensus of the experts who wrote it.

Copyright © 1992 American Psychiatric Association

ALL RIGHTS RESERVED

Manufactured in the United States of America on acid-free paper

95 94 93 92   4 3 2 1

Library of Congress Cataloging-in-Publication Data
Handbook of psychiatric practice in the juvenile court / by the Workgroup
  on Psychiatric Practice in the Juvenile Court,
  Michael G. Kalogerakis, chair
      p.   cm.
  Includes bibliographical references (p.   ) and index.
  ISBN 0-89042-233-8
      1. Forensic psychiatry—United States. 2. Juvenile justice,
  Administration of—United States. 3. Adolescent psychiatry—United
  States. 4. Child psychiatry—United States. I. Kalogerakis, Michael G.
  II. American Psychiatric Association. Workgroup on Psychiatric
  Practice in the Juvenile Court.
  RA1151.H25 1992
  614'.1—dc20   91-23403
                                                                        CIP

British Library Cataloguing in Publication Data
A CIP record is available from the British Library.

HANDBOOK OF PSYCHIATRIC PRACTICE IN THE JUVENILE COURT

To the memory of the Honorable Justine Wise Polier,
vigorous and eloquent defender of children,
and loyal friend and relentless critic of psychiatry
in its long and beleaguered association
with the juvenile justice system

CONTENTS

CONTRIBUTORS

Michael G. Kalogerakis, M.D., Chair
Clinical Professor of Psychiatry
New York University School of Medicine
New York, New York

Carl P. Malmquist, M.D., M.S.
Professor of Social Psychiatry
University of Minnesota
Minneapolis, Minnesota

Sandra G. Nye, J.D., M.S.W.
Assistant Professor of Jurisprudence in Psychiatry
Abraham Lincoln School of Medicine
University of Illinois
Chicago, Illinois

Joseph J. Palombi, M.D.
Clinical Assistant Professor of Psychiatry
Georgetown University School of Medicine
Washington, DC

Kathleen M. Quinn, M.D.
Assistant Professor of Psychiatry
Case Western Reserve Medical School
Cleveland, Ohio

Richard A. Ratner, M.D.
Clinical Professor of Psychiatry and Behavioral Sciences
George Washington University School of Medicine
Washington, DC

Judge W. Don Reader
Stark County Family Court
Canton, Ohio
President, National Council of Juvenile and
  Family Court Judges (1990–1991)

Helen Sacks, M.S.W.
Director, Court Clinic
Superior Court for Juvenile Matters
New Haven, Connecticut

Jane Edgerton
Editorial Consultant
Washington, DC

PREFACE

Responding to a persistent expression of interest from a number of concerned members, the American Psychiatric Association established a Task Force on Juvenile Justice Issues in 1985 under the aegis of the Council on Children, Adolescents, and Their Families. Juvenile justice matters directly affect only a small cadre of psychiatrists, but a far greater number are drawn into court-related issues occasionally and may find themselves lacking the knowledge to deal with the special problems they encounter.

The task force noted that psychiatrists, even those who worked extensively with adolescents, frequently were reluctant to become involved in juvenile court matters. After an early history of rather close collaboration between the law and psychiatry with regard to youth in conflict with society (the child guidance movement grew out of this association), psychiatrists became less and less involved in the juvenile justice system. In part a reflection of diminishing interest in the public sector generally, it was also a sign of growing disillusionment with the juvenile court and with the rehabilitation model that was its guiding principle.

More recently, the increasing level of violence among youth, the regular presence of significant emotional disturbance in youth before the court, the alarming explosion of illicit drug use, the worrisome incidence of child abuse, and the general daily reminders of widespread family disorganization have reaffirmed the need to involve the mental health professions at several points when children and families are before the court. Typically, juvenile and family courts are overwhelmed by both the volume of cases and the lack of resources in most communities. Without the necessary professional expertise to deal with difficult psychiatric questions, they often have no alternative but to settle for unsatisfactory or inappropriate dispositions.

The wish for a greater psychiatric presence in the juvenile courts has become widespread in judicial circles. The task force noted, however, that such participation as currently exists often leaves both the legal and psychiatric professions dissatisfied. Judges and lawyers frequently are unaware of what psychiatry and psychiatrists can and cannot do. Psychiatric evaluations may be lacking in relevance, and too often reports are not responsive to the specialized needs of the court. Barriers to effective communication between the two systems should be fought by both lawyers and psychiatrists. Improving the dialogue by elucidating what information needs to be provided by the psychiatrist appearing in juvenile court and how this is best done is the goal of this book.

Task force members were unanimous in their feeling that improved training for the particular needs of the juvenile justice system would, over time, lead to the development of a network of specially qualified psychiatrists who could better serve that system.* They decided that a handbook for psychiatrists that deals with the specific concerns of the juvenile courts and other segments of the juvenile justice system was needed. To this end, an interdisciplinary workgroup was appointed, the members of which have a wide range of experience—clinical and legal—in juvenile justice. *Handbook of Psychiatric Practice in the Juvenile Court* is the product of their efforts. We hope it will be a useful adjunct to training mental health professionals for work in the juvenile courts, and that it will prove valuable to the legal profession as well.

The Task Force on Juvenile Justice Issues was composed of Edward H. Futterman, M.D., Chair, William M. Buzogany, M.D., Carolyn R. Haynie, M.D., Michael G. Kalogerakis, M.D., and Richard C. Marohn, M.D. The Workgroup on Psychiatric Practice in the Juvenile Court would like to record with great sorrow the untimely passing on March 23, 1991, of Dr. Edward Futterman, guiding spirit of the task force and a major force in establishment of the workgroup.

The generous support of the Kenworthy-Swift Foundation made this undertaking possible and is gratefully acknowledged. The Tappan Foundation provided funds to begin this project and we thank them.

The workgroup commends and thanks Jane Edgerton who served as editorial consultant for the handbook and who provided skillful advice and insight to the project.

Michael G. Kalogerakis, M.D.

---

*Task Force on Juvenile Justice Issues: The psychiatrist and the juvenile justice system. Am J Psychiatry 174:1584–1586, 1990

INTRODUCTION

Michael G. Kalogerakis, M.D.

When America again moves toward more generous programs for its youth, juvenile courts will have a special role to play. They are witness to the consequences of failed policies and practices hurtful to youth. They are in a position to present what they see as constant cases of injuries to youth. They can look beyond individual cases to discover patterns or wrongful injuries to youth, whether inflicted by communities, agencies, or parental failures.

At the same time, the juvenile courts must pursue the daily task of trying youth and making decisions for their future. They must pick up the pieces for individual youths and their parents that have been allowed to fall through the cracks of institutions. They must act as sentinels to protect youth against both overreaching and underdoing on the part of those charged by law to provide preventive and supportive services.[*]

Honorable Justine Wise Polier, New York State Family Court

The world over, children and adolescents in ever-increasing numbers are getting caught up in the juvenile justice system. Some are offenders who have broken the law; many have become unmanageable for their families; others are victims of neglect or abuse by their caretakers; still others may be caught in the middle of a marital breakup in which they become the subjects of a custody dispute. A disproportionate number are from poverty-stricken, inner-city families. All are in trouble. Their basic rights may be in jeopardy, and the majority are experiencing some degree of emotional trauma related to their involvement with the law.

In the United States alone, the juvenile courts handled over 1.3 million cases of delinquency and status offenses (unmanageability) in 1984, the last year for which nationwide statistics are available (1). The cost to the

---

[*]From *Juvenile Justice in Double Jeopardy: The Distanced Community and Vengeful Retribution* by Justine Wise Polier, p. 162. Reprinted with permission of Lawrence Erlbaum Associates, Inc.

nation in dollars runs into the billions; the cost in human misery is immeasurable.

Delinquency, affecting as it does the young, tears at the very fabric of society. It is without doubt the most corrosive social force we know. Sadly, it is too often refractory to the most intensive rehabilitative efforts.

Fifty percent of those appearing in juvenile court on charges of delinquency or status offenses have been before the court previously, often several times (1). Clearly, there is a high risk that once in the system, an adolescent will remain its captive for the remainder of his or her juvenile period. With each appearance in court, there is usually further deterioration and diminishing hope that a youth will become a functioning member of society. The personality damage may be even more pervasive when the child is a victim of child abuse.

The medical and psychiatric needs of this population have been amply documented (2) and are significantly greater than those of the general population. The American Medical Association has taken note of this and, in a recent initiative, addressed the segment of this population that ends up either in detention or incarcerated (3). It has urged medical and psychiatric organizations, as well as the government, to attend to the special needs of this group. They should work with related interested organizations such as the National Commission on Correctional Health Care, the National Council of Juvenile and Family Court Judges, and other groups.

The present endeavor by the American Psychiatric Association focuses on the portal of entry into the juvenile justice system—the juvenile court. This book examines in detail the role that psychiatry and other mental health professions are called on to play with regard to children, adolescents, and their families who turn up in court referred by the police, the schools, social services, child protective services, and others. (However, it does not address custody matters that are often handled in domestic relations or state supreme court [4–6].)

The need in court is first to identify and diagnose psychiatric illness and second to develop recommendations for the court based on the evaluation. To do this competently and in a manner that responds to the particular needs of the court while respecting the rights of the individuals who are under legal scrutiny is a major challenge to the mental health professions involved in forensic work. At present, such competence exists only sparsely, leaving many juvenile courts poorly served, if served at all.

Competence in forensic child and adolescent psychiatry requires knowledge that is not acquired routinely in the course of a general psychiatry residency or even most training programs in child psychiatry. The psychiatric issues that are likely to arise in court, the characteristics of the specific patient population, the statutory requirements that determine how the court must operate, normal procedures in the court, the nuances of handling oneself in an adversarial system, familiarity with the local laws, and availability of services together represent a collection of technical skills and information for which some supplementary training is essential (7). Although specific training in forensic child psychiatry already exists, it remains limited (see Chapter 17). The enormous needs of the juvenile and family courts will not be met in the foreseeable future (if ever) by the comparatively few graduates of these intensive training programs. Less ambitious efforts to educate the many mental health professionals who are called on to render service to the court are appropriate.

The chapters that follow address in turn the basic background information needed for an understanding of the juvenile justice system and the technical aspects of serving as a mental health expert in the court. To avoid repetition, a number of terms are used interchangeably: mental health expert, clinician, forensic specialist, examiner, evaluator, etc. The reader will remember that, in different jurisdictions, the mental health professional providing the service to the court may be a psychiatrist, a clinical psychologist, or, less commonly, a psychiatric social worker. In keeping with the concept of a handbook, the emphasis throughout this book is practical rather than theoretical, specific and detailed rather than general. The appendixes provide more extensive information than the body of the text on such matters as writing a report, contracts, and other useful items.

REFERENCES

1. U.S. Department of Justice: Juvenile Court Statistics, 1984. Washington, DC, Office of Juvenile Justice and Delinquency Prevention, 1987
2. American Medical Association: Common Health Problems of Juveniles in Correctional Facilities. Chicago, IL, American Medical Association, 1979
3. American Medical Association Council on Scientific Affairs: Health status of detained and incarcerated youth. JAMA 263:987–991, 1990
4. Gardner RA: Family Evaluation in Child Custody Litigation. Cresskill, NJ, Creative Therapy, 1982
5. Skaste D: Child Custody Evaluation: A Practical Guide. Beverly Hills, CA, Sage, 1985
6. Weithorn LA (ed): Psychology and Child Custody Determination: Knowledge, Roles and Expertise. Lincoln, University of Nebraska Press, 1987
7. Task Force on Juvenile Justice Issues: The psychiatrist and the juvenile justice system. Am J Psychiatry 174:1584–1586, 1990

CHAPTER 2

HISTORY OF THE JUVENILE COURT

Helen Sacks, M.S.W.
Judge W. Don Reader

Two disparate philosophical themes emerge out of a developmental review of the juvenile court's history in the United States. One theme is of a court of law for children with legal and procedural safeguards; the other is that of the juvenile court as a social welfare agency with psychosocial remedies, attempting to reform wayward youth. "Should we punish?" or "should we treat?" are questions that define the ambivalence and characterize the difficulties the court has had in discharging its diverse roles. According to Whitebread and Heilman (1), "the tension between rehabilitation and punishment is the most powerful dynamic at work in the juvenile system" (p. 286). From the beginning, this struggle has dominated, and continues to dominate, all other issues in the court.

The juvenile justice movement began in the early nineteenth century when the linkages between poverty and delinquency caught the attention of a group of philanthropists committed to religious charity. Taking the initiative as moral stewards of their community, this group of early reformers examined this connection and recommended changes in policy and legislation, especially with respect to the housing of children in adult jails. Before the juvenile justice movement, children were treated as chattels of adults without any rights, and if found guilty of a crime, they were sentenced as any adult would be. This reform group did not accept the common notion that such harsh conditions would result in the rehabilitation of delinquents. In fact, many believed that the conditions of the adult prisons led juries and judges to acquit the young rather than send them to such inhuman places. They envisioned a special prison for wayward youths that would emphasize education, industry, and moral training (2).

The first of these youth prisons, the New York City House of Refuge, was opened in 1825. Within a few years, other houses of refuge that accepted children convicted of crimes as well as destitute youth were established. These facilities were advanced as preventative institutions designed to accept children of unfit parents. The Pennsylvania Supreme

Court in *Ex Parte Crouse* (1838) stated "the object of charity is reformation by training of inmates: by imbuing their minds with principles of morality and religion: by furnishing them with a means to earn a living, and, above all, by separating them from the corrupting influences of improper associates. To this end, may not the natural parents when unequal to the task of education, or unworthy of it, be superseded by the *parens patriae* or common community?" (3). This case appears to be the first application in American law of the legal doctrine of *parens patriae*, the state acting on behalf of the juvenile, which began the development of the virtually unrestrained powers of later juvenile courts.

In 1899, the state of Illinois adopted the first juvenile code, which established the country's first juvenile court, radically altering the way children were dealt with in court by imposing the overriding objective of rehabilitation. The concern of this law was the character of the offender rather than the nature of the offense, reflecting and responding to the developing "child savers" movement. This movement was attempting to "save" children of working-class immigrants from what were considered to be the undesirable elements of their class and culture. Because the state's emphasis was on rehabilitation, not punishment, there was no need for the formal protection of due process. Further developments based on this philosophy included informal, closed proceedings resulting in sealed records to avoid stigmatizing juveniles. Dispositions evolved based on the medical model of diagnosing social ills. The court's key considerations were who needed treatment and who could profit from it. This opened the doors of the courts to the mental health profession, which would become the major force in carrying out this mandate.

By 1918 the reform movement was well accepted, and many states officially enacted juvenile court laws in their endeavor to help, protect, and rehabilitate juveniles rather than to punish them. The laws provided for the original procedure of separate hearings but also began to include probation services, social history investigations, and when possible, mental and physical examinations for delinquents to be used by the court in the decision-making process. These efforts were in the service of attempting to diagnose and treat the delinquent as well as to collect data to establish the principles of prevention. The earliest court clinic was established in 1909 by Dr. William Healy, who used an array of psychiatric techniques to understand the meaning of the delinquent's behavior. Other clinics were established, representing new ideas in child development from the fields of psychiatry, psychology, and social work.

During the 1920s, as the child guidance movement began to develop expertise, professional mental health services available through the courts were expanded. Social workers and probation officers were now trained to divert delinquents away from institutions that were deemed too restrictive. Instead probation officers placed the youths on probation, supervised family life through home visits, and involved the school and social and welfare agencies. The court at this time was given jurisdiction over children who had committed adult crimes or who exhibited noncriminal or status offense behavior. These status offenders included truants, runaway youth, children beyond the control of their parents, and those deemed incorrigible. The proceedings of the courtroom had little to do with law, and the role of lawyers was not prominent.

The cornerstone of the juvenile court philosophy of individualized treatment allowed for further changes during the 1930s and 1940s. The moral superiority and authoritarianism of the child savers movement of an earlier time were replaced by a psychosocial model of adjustment. New theories of treatment arose relating to emotional and personality problems with a focus on the youth's inner life, superseding previous emphases on detrimental environmental influences (4). This new focus was a marked shift away from one of the earlier beliefs of the court: that the child was not responsible for his or her behavior and that behavioral problems reflected social conditions. The basic assumption about the ease of rehabilitation also fell by the wayside. The introduction of psychotherapeutic modalities, such as behavior modification and psychoanalytically oriented approaches that related delinquency to unconscious conflict and poorly controlled inner drives, seemed to have little effect on the rate of recidivism.

By the 1940s, sociological theories of deviance had become central to the understanding of delinquency. Antisocial behavior was seen as a response to different subcultures developing in urban ethnic groups that had moral and organizational patterns different from those of the dominant social order. Research and clinical investigations continued as psychological, cultural, and biological theories of behavioral disturbances were explored further. Efforts were focused on analyzing delinquent behavior more scientifically; an example is the multifactor scale formulated by Eleanor and Sheldon Glueck (5). This instrument was believed to be predictive of delinquent behavior. These ideas ushered in the movement to use psychiatrists as professionals who could modify children's behavior. Because the courts were not able to provide the array of services required to fill both the judicial and therapeutic functions, the challenge of redirecting wayward youth was only partially addressed.

A new era of juvenile justice began in the 1950s, due in part to the greater mobility of juveniles, the growing problem of drug use, and a marked increase of violent youth gangs. Small towns across America had not been seriously affected by delinquency, which was most often committed close to offenders' urban homes and away from suburban, middle-class communities. Many segments of society were vulnerable now, and critics of the juvenile justice system became more vocal and organized.

Their potent attacks ranged from accusations of excessive judicial leniency with violent offenders to excessive harshness in depriving female status offenders of liberties. Other criticisms related to the stigmatization of youths, discriminatory sentencing practices, and child abuse occurring in juvenile correction facilities. The major thrust for change came with the belief that the treatment model of deterring delinquency had failed, and the juvenile court had not fulfilled its promise. The decline in the era of rehabilitation had begun.

The Supreme Court decision in *Kent v. United States* (1966) (6) took note of the shortcomings of the juvenile justice system. Justice Fortas wrote that "there must be grounds for concern that the child receives the worst of both worlds; that he gets neither the protection accorded to adults nor the solicitous care and rejuvenative treatment postulated for children." One year later, in 1967, the Supreme Court decided a juvenile case that had a profound impact on juvenile law and children's rights (7). Gerald Gault, a 15-year-old Arizona youth who was arrested and charged with making lewd telephone calls, was committed to the state industrial school until adulthood. The maximum penalty for an adult using obscene language over the telephone was a 2-month jail term. This landmark decision found that juveniles before the court were entitled to the same protections accorded to adults, including the right to counsel, the right to notice of specific charges of the offense, the right to confront and cross-examine a witness, the right to remain silent, and the right to subpoena witnesses in defense (omitted was the right to trial by jury). *In re Gault* established reform in the juvenile justice system, prompting federal legislation that accorded juveniles the aforementioned rights in court hearings. An additional procedural protection was added in a subsequent decision by the court in 1970, *In re Winship* (8), which established the burden of proof "beyond a reasonable doubt" in juvenile proceedings. The juvenile court now had defined legal standards as well as an existing social welfare philosophy—not always compatible obligations. The debate continued.

In 1967, President Johnson's Commission on Law Enforcement and the Administration of Justice made known its findings. The juvenile court was criticized for its failure to meet the needs of delinquent youth, with the acknowledgment that the court had not been provided with adequate personnel or services to fulfill its mandate. The report warned against the pendulum swinging too far away from the rehabilitation model toward retribution. It made a forceful recommendation for preventive community services for "at risk" youth, as well as for those already drawn into the court system.

The social activism of the 1960s was also reflected in the activism of legislative bodies. By July 1974, Congress enacted the Juvenile Justice and Delinquency Prevention Act, which allocated funds for programs that emphasized community-based treatment and prevention (9). It established the Office of Juvenile Justice and Delinquency Prevention to oversee these programs. This influential legislation, which called for decriminalization, deinstitutionalization, and the elimination of court authority over status offenders, created a furor. There were those who believed that the courts' authority was essential in dealing with status offenders, but this new approach was hailed by the civil libertarians who advocated the separation of criminal and noncriminal youth in juvenile court. The debate also continued over deinstitutionalization or the closing down of juvenile correctional facilities. These were to be replaced with smaller, more open local facilities. The federal incentives to states to implement these legislative reforms were inadequate.

These reforms were also part of the recommendations in the Juvenile Justice Standards Project, a major, 23-volume study completed by the American Bar Association and Institute of Judicial Administration, usually referred to as the ABA/IJA Standards (10). Their model of the new juvenile court emphasized the importance of constitutional rights and due process, even to the extent of jury trials, and completely rejected the rehabilitative philosophy. The standards recommended the "five D's": due process, (just) deserts (determinate sentences), diversion, deinstitutionalization, and decriminalization. Critics of the standards emanated from both the right and the left of the political spectrum, even within the membership of the American Bar Association. National professional organizations such as the National Council of Juvenile and Family Court Judges and the National District Attorneys Association stated their positions, most of which were in opposition to the adoption of the standards. Further criticism of the Juvenile Justice Standards project came from the American Psychiatric Association (11). This group argued against the abandonment of the rehabilitative model, believing that the crucial differences between adults and children warranted a separate system that addresses the developmental needs of children and adolescents. The American Psychiatric Association also advocated the retention of court jurisdiction over the status offenders. To abandon these offenders without alternative programs in place would leave a substantial group of noncriminal delinquents unattended. The American Psychiatric Association reaffirmed psychiatry's role in the juvenile justice system and supported reforms that would reflect differences between children and adults.

The freedom cry of the 1960s spawned the explosion of runaways in the 70s. Shelters and residential services were already in short supply and thus were not able to handle the onslaught of thousands of runaway children. Community preventive programs, called for by the legislation, did not offer enough opportunities in job development or independent living and lacked coordination. Advocates for reform became disillusioned. Support for the removal of status offenders from court jurisdiction began to decline, and the appropriateness of the federal government's role in regulating local practices was questioned. Organized youth gangs were on the rise, and increasing violence committed by juveniles was reported.

In 1984, the National Advisory Committee for Juvenile Justice and Delinquency Prevention sharply criticized the previous policy initiative of deinstitutionalization and diversion (12). The committee argued for a new federal focus on serious juvenile offenders with emphasis on deterrence, fixed sentencing, and incarceration of youths. State legislators responded, passing laws allowing juveniles to be transferred to adult courts. Some states legislated automatic transfer or waiver laws requiring that a youngster who committed a serious and violent crime be transferred automatically to adult court. In addition to this wave of "get tough" legislation, the United States Supreme Court's majority opinion in *Schall v. Martin* (1984) (13) was a clear indication of a more restrictive attitude toward children's rights. The Court held that the preventive detention of juveniles before trial was a legitimate state action to prevent pretrial crimes. However, the status offender problem remained. Many states had legislated different labels for the noncriminal offender (e.g., "persons in need of supervision" [PINS] and "children in need of supervision" [CHINS]) and the separation of status offenders from delinquent youths in juvenile facilities as required by the Juvenile Justice Act. In some states, however, the court did not have the power to enforce treatment recommendations. Where the state has granted that power, the court has been able to involve families in the rehabilitation of their children. The use of such power has been sharply debated, with some observers submitting that the autonomy and privacy of a youth must be respected and treatment implemented by a voluntary contract.

These concerns heralded the children's rights movement, a strong factor in juvenile proceedings during the 1980s. Because the protections of procedural due process had been established, legal activists began to take the position that treatment recommendations were too intrusive, impinging on children's civil liberties. During these years violent crime increased significantly, with escalation of drug selling and drug abuse. The popular response has been a strong call for harsher punishments. The government's fiscal problems resulted in serious cutbacks in federally funded community services during these years. This lack of funding has made rehabilitative programs underfunded or scarce.

In addition, juvenile courts have been affected by a significant increase in cases involving dependent, neglected, and abused children; children born addicted to drugs; children suffering from fetal alcohol syndrome; and children infected with the AIDS virus—all entering the system soon after birth. Complaints involving sexually abused children have quadrupled in the same time period. Termination of parental rights in cases of abuse and foster care placement or adoption loom large on the horizon.

In spite of all the ongoing controversies and difficulties, the role of the mental health professional in the juvenile court has remained important. Regardless of the ascendant philosophy during the evolution of the juvenile court and despite the present trend toward a more legalistic model, the psychiatrist's expertise has been sought continuously to provide evaluations and recommendations for treatment in the juvenile justice system.

REFERENCES

1. Whitebread CH, Heilman J: An overview of the law of juvenile delinquency. Behavioral Sciences and the Law 6(3):285–305, 1988
2. Platt AM: The Child Savers, The Invention of Delinquency. Chicago, IL, University of Chicago Press, 1969
3. Ex Parte Crouse, 1838
4. Giallombardo R (ed): Juvenile Delinquency, A Book of Readings, 2nd Edition. New York, John Wiley, 1972
5. Glueck S, Glueck E: Unraveling Juvenile Delinquency. New York, Commonwealth Fund, 1950
6. Kent v United States, 383 US 541, 1966
7. In re Gault, 387 US 1, 1967
8. In re Winship, 397 US 358, 1970
9. Juvenile Justice Delinquency Prevention Act of 1974, 88 Stat 1109
10. American Bar Association: Juvenile Justice Standards: Summary and Analysis. Cambridge, MA, Ballinger Press, 1977
11. American Psychiatric Association: Response to Juvenile Justice Standards Project of the ABA/IJA. Washington, DC, American Psychiatric Association, 1978
12. National Advisory Committee for Juvenile Justice and Delinquency Prevention: Serious Juvenile Crime: A Redirected Federal Effort. Washington, DC, U.S. Department of Justice, Office of Juvenile Justice and Delinquency Prevention, 1984
13. Schall v Martin, 467 US 253, 1984

PROCEDURES IN THE JUVENILE COURT

Helen Sacks, M.S.W.
Judge W. Don Reader

Juvenile courts' jurisdiction and procedure differ widely throughout the United States. Courts derive their authority from state legislatures. In the majority of the states, the court's jurisdiction extends to age 18 years, whereas some states limit jurisdiction to ages 17, 16, or younger. A youth who commits an act that would be a crime if committed by an adult is brought before the juvenile court as a delinquent. A youth who commits an act that would be prohibited by law, but is not necessarily a crime (e.g., truancy, running away, incorrigibility—actions generally referred to as status offenses) may also be brought to the jurisdiction of the juvenile court. In addition, the court's jurisdiction extends to children found to be dependent, neglected, and physically or sexually abused. In some states, the juvenile or family court will also hear custody cases, although more often these matters are dealt with in a separate court such as domestic relations or state supreme court. Delinquent referrals, abuse and neglect matters, and status offenses are each heard separately. In all of these matters the juvenile court's jurisdiction is exclusive. In cases involving crimes that adults commit against children, jurisdiction may be concurrent with other courts (1).

INTAKE PHASE

Juvenile courts receive delinquency referrals from many different sources, including parents, police officers, victims, and schools (see Figure 3–1). The local social service agency is the most frequent referral source for the dependent, neglect, and abuse cases. The delinquency referrals usually come to the court's intake department by way of information (e.g., from parents) or official complaint (e.g., the police). The intake staff (in many courts the probation officer) examines the referral report to see what type of crime is alleged to have been committed and tries to determine whether this is a first offense or there is a prior record. A decision is made to handle

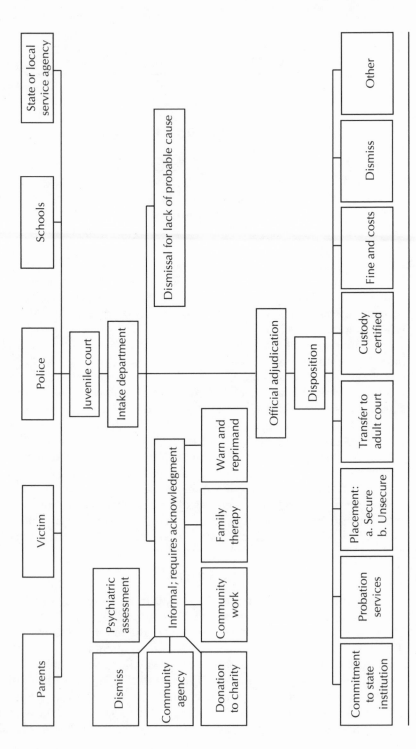

Figure 3–1. Juvenile court flow chart

the case either formally or informally. If the case is handled informally, or "out of court," the judge is not involved. The hearing is conducted by the intake officer, and an attempt is made to help the youth accept responsibility for the alleged act and give him or her a chance to eliminate the delinquent behavior without imposition of judicial sanctions. This is known as diversion. For the procedure to be used, the child must acknowledge commission of the act. The act cannot be a serious crime involving violence. In some states, it is sufficient to agree not to contest the allegations. Disposition at this point may include dismissal of charges, a reprimand, restitution in the form of a donation to a charity or payment for property destroyed, a community work project, or referral to a social service agency or a mental health resource for child or family therapy.

ADJUDICATORY PHASE

If the intake department determines that the complaint or information must be processed formally, the case is set for arraignment before a judge. At this time due process requires that the youth be represented by counsel. When there are financial limitations, this service will be provided by a public defender. Otherwise, private counsel is appointed for the youth. In some cases where the parents strongly oppose their child's wishes, they may retain their own counsel separate and distinct from that of the child. If the youth admits to the charge, there is no need for a trial and a dispositional hearing will be held. Should the youth deny the delinquency complaint, the matter is set for trial. This is known in juvenile court as the adjudicatory hearing. At this time, each side presents evidence and witnesses and the judge makes a decision as to the guilt or innocence based on the facts. A psychiatric evaluation may be requested at this point if the facts seem to warrant it. If the youth is found not to have committed the acts with which he or she is charged, the case is dismissed. If the allegations are proven, the child is adjudicated delinquent or a status offender, and the court enters the dispositional phase of the procedure.

DISPOSITIONAL PHASE

The dispositional phase is the heartbeat of the juvenile court and represents the major difference between juvenile court and adult court procedure. It is at disposition that individualized justice that focuses on rehabilitation, which is the hallmark of the juvenile justice system, is most clearly in evidence. To maximize the court's options and effectiveness at disposition, any and all information relative to the youth should be available to the judge. Such information includes but is not limited to the following: family history, school records, prior offense history, past psychiatric or psychological evaluations, assessment of alcohol and drug use, and current psychiatric or psychological evaluations that had been ordered at the time of adjudication.

The most troubling problem at disposition is the lack of quality therapeutic residential and community programs that offer a real chance of rehabilitation. Assuming that the court does have resources available, the following dispositions will be considered (see also Chapter 9):

1. Commitment to the juvenile justice or the correctional system
2. Probation, generally up to 2 years
3. Supervision rarely exceeding 3 months
4. Community placement, such as in a group home
5. Waiver or transfer to adult criminal court
6. Custody to a certified state agency other than the juvenile justice agency, such as the department of social services, department of mental health, or department of mental retardation

Any placement ordered may include family involvement and family therapy, if this is deemed necessary. Under the terms of probation, much creative programming can be implemented. Examples include requiring a restitution plan, involvement in community work programs, referral to community mental health centers for the child and the family, attending meetings of Alcoholics Anonymous or Narcotics Anonymous, receiving special tutoring for the learning disabled, assignment to a Big Brother or Big Sister, and referrals to counseling programs focused on special problems, such as those for sex offenders. When a child is placed in the custody of a state agency, based on the findings of the court that the child is neglected or uncared for, the court generally requires a plan for reunification of the family with periodic reviews to ensure that reasonable efforts are being made by the agency toward this end, with the participation of the parents.

The foregoing represent the standard or usual procedures in the juvenile court. There are others that may be invoked in specified circumstances and at different points in the proceedings. These include waiver or transfer of jurisdiction to the adult criminal court, pretrial detention, competency determinations, and use of the insanity defense. The first two procedures will be described here; the latter two will be dealt with in Chapter 5.

WAIVER

In the event of an extremely serious delinquency matter and before the case is put up for adjudication, the court can order a transfer or waiver hearing to determine whether the case should be heard in the juvenile setting or be transferred to the adult criminal court. This waiver becomes a consideration in most states when the child is 15 years of age or older and has committed an act that would be a serious felony if committed by an adult, and the court has established *probable cause,* i.e., the preliminary determination that the youth probably committed the act for which he or she is charged. A further determination must be made regarding whether the youth would be amenable to treatment in a state or private facility designed for the care or treatment of minors and whether or not such placement would pose a serious threat to the safety of the community. If deemed inappropriate for juvenile placement, the youth may be transferred to the adult court where adult sentencing procedures apply and more restrictive institutions would be available. As a result of recent Supreme Court decisions (2–4), sentencing in that case would include the possibility of the death penalty, a disposition not available in juvenile court.

DETENTION

Another special procedure not infrequently implemented in juvenile court is *detention.* In this procedure, a youth who has been brought to court on a delinquency charge may be confined to a secure or nonsecure facility rather than being sent home while the court hears the case. The period of time is quite variable and depends on the court calendar and the complexity of the case. In order to make use of this option, one of several conditions must be present and must be shown to exist at a detention hearing held with the parents present within 72 hours after the youth is placed. The conditions for the use of detention are:

1. *There is a strong probability that the youth will run away prior to the court hearing.* A parent may advise the court that the youngster leaves home repeatedly for long periods. The parent may be unable to assure the court that the youngster will remain at home and appear in court when needed. At times, specific information is reported to the court, detailing plans of the youth to leave the community.
2. *There is reason to believe that the juvenile will commit other offenses harmful to self or others before the court hearing on the charges.* This is especially likely when the youth has had a series of recent adjudications or referrals to court. Often, such a spree or cluster of delinquencies connects to a crisis in the life of the child or to a traumatic event occurring in the family.
3. *There is reasonable cause to believe that staying home will not be safe or in the child's best interests, or will pose a hazard to those in the community because of the dangerous or violent nature of the alleged act.* Included in this category

are children charged with "serious juvenile offenses" as designated by
state statute, which may differ in various parts of the country. These
especially violent or serious charges may include murder, arson, rape,
kidnapping, armed robbery, first and second degree assault, and (recently added) sale of narcotics. There may be some concern that the child
might repeat the delinquent behavior, as well as concern for the harm
that could come to the youth because of threats from people in the
community. This condition for detention also applies to a child over 14
years of age who is charged with a serious juvenile offense, meets the
criteria for transfer to adult criminal court, and awaits a hearing on the
matter.

4. *There is a need to hold the child for another jurisdiction (another court).*
   Out-of-state runaways, youths from another state apprehended in a
   delinquent act, or youths wanted in another state for a pending delinquency matter may be held in detention as decreed by the interstate
   compact laws.

5. *The child has failed to appear in the juvenile court in the past.* Dysfunctional
   families, unable to organize their lives, may frequently and repeatedly
   miss court appearances with their child. In some instances, there has
   been an erosion of the court authority that enabled the family to ignore
   the summons. In other cases, parents do not respond appropriately to
   the seriousness of their child's delinquent behavior.

At the detention hearing, if a judge decides that the child must remain
in the detention center until the adjudicatory hearing, the child is usually
sent to the center closest to his or her home. Typically, another detention
hearing is held every 15 days until the court determines that detention is
no longer required.

Pretrial detention has been a controversial issue. Legal advocates for
children's rights voice concern that the act may violate a youth's constitutional right of presumption of innocence. The Supreme Court in *Schall v.
Martin* (5) upheld the constitutionality of detaining a youth before adjudication when there is a serious danger that further delinquency may occur
before the hearing on the delinquency petition. The court's rationale was
that placement of a youth in detention protects both the delinquent and
the community. States have responded differently to the constitutional
issues when considering the argument. The requirement of holding a
hearing to determine whether there is probable cause before allowing
pretrial detention is debated. Whether a juvenile has a right to bail and the
right to trial by jury (denied by the court in *McKeiver v. Pennsylvania* [6])
are further constitutional concerns that receive support from some who
want to criminalize the juvenile justice system. Mental health professionals challenge that position, questioning whether more procedural protec-

tions will advance the mental health objectives that are associated with the rehabilitative juvenile justice model. There is greater consensus with respect to the harm done when a youth remains in a detention facility for a long period of time before adjudication. A long delay is detrimental to a juvenile's emotional health and psychological well-being, and there is little disagreement as to the right to a speedy adjudication. Utilizing pretrial detention raises the question of whether the facility is appropriate for those remanded and whether the various groups involved should be differentiated. Most agree that children should be separated from adult criminals and that delinquents should be segregated from status offenders. Some states have a range of facilities, from secure closed settings to open shelters, that allow for suitable placements of each category of offender.

Pretrial detention will continue to have its detractors as well as its supporters. As with many other controversial issues that afflict the juvenile court, a balance must be struck between the restrictions of personal freedom and the danger of doing harm to self or others. At various points during the procedures described, from intake through disposition and in relationship to waiver and detention, a mental health evaluation may be requested by the court. The circumstances that may lead to such a request and what is expected of the psychiatrist called on to perform the evaluation are considered in Chapter 5.

REFERENCES

1. Whitebread CH, Heilman J: An overview of the law of juvenile delinquency. Behavioral Sciences and the Law 6(3):285–305, 1988
2. Thompson v Oklahoma, 101 L.Ed.2nd 702, 1988
3. Stanford v Kentucky, 87-5765, 1989
4. Wilkins v Missouri, 87-6026, 1989
5. Schall v Martin, 467 US 253, 1984
6. McKeiver v Pennsylvania, 403 US 528, 1971

CHAPTER 4

PARTICIPANTS IN THE JUVENILE COURT

Sandra G. Nye, J.D., M.S.W.

CAST OF CHARACTERS

The courtroom is staffed by a number of functionaries, the roles of whom may not be entirely comprehensible without a "scorecard" to identify the players. They will vary from one jurisdiction to another and sometimes from one courtroom to another in the same jurisdiction, but the following will serve to introduce the newcomer to the general scheme of things.

The *judge* is responsible for administering the courtroom and running the trials and hearings. He or she may be elected or appointed, depending on the jurisdiction. Although it was not always the case, now all judges are lawyers. Most have had practical experience in a juvenile court. Politics plays a part in the selection and retention of judges whether they are elected or appointed. This sometimes makes judges subject to political and media pressure. In some jurisdictions, juvenile court judges are elected specifically to that post. In others, they may be appointed to the court by the chief judge. Rarely do juvenile judges come to their posts with any specialized training or background other than general legal education. It is incumbent on experts participating in juvenile proceedings to provide to the judge in each case all the factual and theoretical bases to enable him or her to comprehend and utilize the clinical material presented.

The role of the judge in the trial process includes conducting the proceedings, ruling on the evidence (what is or is not admissible), making determinations as to the law and its application in the case, and, unless there is a jury, making a determination as to the facts. The judge is responsible for determining placement of the child while the proceedings pend, making such interim orders as are necessary to the conduct of the case (e.g., ordering clinical examinations), and making the disposition of the case if there has been a finding of delinquency, dependency, neglect, or abuse.

The *court clerk* runs the business end of the juvenile court. He or she keeps the schedule, is responsible for seeing that documents and court orders are entered into the record, and calls the cases. The court clerk is the interface between the judge and the legal representatives.

The *bailiff* keeps order in the juvenile court and is often a deputy sheriff or other police officer. He or she is responsible for the behavior of people in the court room, the physical protection of the judge, and when necessary, the physical management of the defendant—guarding or escorting the youth to or from the lock-up. The bailiff may be armed.

The *guardian ad litem* (GAL) is usually an attorney. A GAL is often appointed for minors (or in other proceedings for any party who lacks the legal or actual competence to represent himself or herself) and has the duty of representing to the court the best interests of the child. Some jurisdictions require a GAL in all juvenile proceedings. The precise functions of the GAL will vary from one jurisdiction to another. It may be useful to inquire about the specific responsibilities in each situation. Usually the GAL is viewed as the eyes and ears of the court. The GAL determines what is in the best interests of the child and so advises the court. The attorney representing the child, on the other hand, is bound to present to the court his or her client's views and wishes, whether or not they are in the client's best interests. The GAL is not bound by the wishes or instructions of the client. The court looks to the GAL for guidance, so he or she is extremely influential in the outcome. Therefore, it is important that the GAL fully understand the clinical aspects of the case.

Some jurisdictions have a *protective services agency liaison* assigned to the juvenile court room. This person may act as a representative of the agency to inform the court what the possibilities are and to receive the court's orders about the agency's responsibilities in a given case.

The *juvenile probation officer* may be responsible for intake and pre-intake screening of cases for diversion. Sometimes the probation officer is required to participate in adjudication by conducting certain investigative tasks and presenting information to the court. After adjudication and as part of the disposition, he or she is usually responsible for conducting a social investigation and advising the court about facts and conditions bearing on the disposition. The clinical expert can have a tremendous impact at this point, offering information and recommendations. If the child is made a ward of the court and not institutionalized, the probation officer will be in charge of monitoring her or his behavior, treatment (if any), and progress. If the child violates the terms of probation, the probation officer is obliged to bring that information to the court for further proceedings. In some jurisdictions, probation officers are required to have education in social work or other related areas. In other jurisdictions, this may not be a requirement. Often, it is useful for the clinical expert to ascertain the level of training and education of the probation officer so that he or she is certain that the necessary clinical facts and concepts are fully understood and utilized in the probation report.

The *prosecutor* may be called the *state's attorney, district attorney,* or some other similar name. His or her duty is to present the case on behalf of "the people" and against the respondent or defendant. The objective of the prosecutor is to prove the allegations contained in the petition and to convince the judge to enter findings and order a disposition in accordance therewith.

Usually the county or state prosecutor's office will use the juvenile court as a training ground for its new lawyers. Often, the juvenile court prosecutor will be relatively inexperienced and may have little or no commitment to children or their interests. Often prosecutors are political or patronage appointees who have taken their positions to learn trial skills and make the political connections that they intend to use to launch their careers in other fields of law. The personal goal of the juvenile court prosecutor may very well be to make his or her reputation, pay the "dues," and be transferred to higher profile assignments or be hired into a lucrative private practice as quickly as possible.

The *public defender* is the defense counterpart of the prosecutor. He or she may be a full-time public employee or may be a private practitioner hired on a part-time basis. Again, political or patronage connections often play a part in obtaining such jobs, and lawyers often take them as a way into a legal career or a means of supporting a young or flagging private practice. The juvenile court is often the training arena for new public defenders, just as it is for prosecutors, and the same economic and other constraints that apply to the prosecutors will also apply to the public defenders.

A respondent or defendant who is unable to afford competent private counsel is at the mercy of the public defender. Needless to say, many public defenders are dedicated, highly competent attorneys who are committed to their client's well-being. The risk, however, of falling into the hands of an untried, unskilled, uncaring practitioner who wants nothing more than not to be bothered and to be practicing elsewhere is very real.

The role of the defense attorney, whether the public defender or privately retained counsel, is to vigorously put forth the client's position—in other words, to win the case. Often, what the client (whether the child or a parent) wants is diametrically opposite to what is in the child's best interests. It may be frustrating and enraging to the mental health professional, who clearly sees a child's needs and the opportunity offered by a juvenile court experience to at least attempt to meet those needs, to be opposed and thwarted by an attorney who simply wants to get the charges dismissed or court intervention in the client's life minimized.

The mental health professional working in the juvenile justice system has a great opportunity, as well as a heavy responsibility, to provide meaningful information and assistance to the court in understanding and arriving at a conclusion that is in the child's best interests. It is in the nature of the work, however, that the mental health professional may be forced into a lonely position between prosecution and defense, neither of whom may be happy with that position. Sometimes, but not always, the GAL is the psychiatrist's ally in looking not to win a conviction or acquittal, but to support the child's best interests.

Publicity may be hard to come by in juvenile court, and it is publicity that makes legal careers more quickly than anything else. In the occasional highly publicized case, then, the best interests of the child may be lost in the shuffle. Many prosecutors' and public defenders' offices pay low salaries and expressly or tacitly permit their legal staffs to engage in private practice as moonlighting. In many jurisdictions, court may be over by early or mid-afternoon, and the prosecutor or public defender may be anxious to leave for other professional activities elsewhere. On the other hand, in some jurisdictions, the caseload is so heavy and the prosecutor's or public defender's office is so understaffed that the lawyers have no time for personal growth or opportunity; may be severely overextended, exhausted, and frustrated; and thus are depressed or angry, cynical, and burned out.

Thus preparation and availability for case discussions with the prosecutor or public defender may be limited. These facts are known to the bar and other court personnel and are important factors in understanding what is going on in the handling of any case. It is not unknown for the psychiatrist who has been hired as a court expert to end up, for better or worse, as the informal personal therapist to the court. The opportunities inherent in such a situation to render genuine service to children, as well as to professional colleagues and the court system, ought not to be overlooked.

It must be remembered that although prosecution and defense may be bitter enemies before the bench, and the judge and other court personnel may seem remote or uninterested, they are all part of the same working system. It is not unusual for them to close ranks against an outsider or a perceived threat to the system's homeostasis. It behooves the clinician who wishes to operate in the system to spend some time observing its interpersonal dynamics, as well as learning the formal context in which these dynamics take place. Sociologically, psychologically, and anthropologically, a juvenile court is a fascinating phenomenon.

CHAPTER 5

ROLE OF THE PSYCHIATRIST

Richard A. Ratner, M.D.

In Chapter 3 a general outline of the workings of the juvenile justice system was presented, describing the stages in the process by which a child or teenager who becomes the object of court concern reaches an appropriate disposition. At many points along the way the expertise and involvement of a psychiatrist may be not only useful but even crucial to the court's ability to act wisely and in the best interests of the young person.

Although all juvenile courts confront the same problems, each state has its own unique set of laws and procedures for addressing those problems. In some states, for example, mental health examinations are not allowed before adjudication, whereas in other states they are common (1). A few states recognize a not guilty by reason of insanity (NGBRI) plea for juveniles, whereas others do not. The agency responsible for juveniles in one state will have a different name from that of an agency doing the same job in another state and may fit under a different branch of state government. Although there is broad overlap regarding the powers of the bench, different states give differing amounts of power and control to judges.

In spite of this variation among jurisdictions, the same kinds of issues must be addressed by the courts of each jurisdiction at more or less the same points in the proceedings. Consequently, the types of situations in which psychiatrists are consulted will be outlined, leaving it to the reader to apply the information for use in his or her own state.

The issues that must be addressed at one juncture are usually quite different from those that arise at another. Depending on the stage of the proceedings, for example, consultation may be requested to consider such disparate issues as diagnosis, competency to stand trial, potential for rehabilitation, dangerousness, or criminal responsibility. In cases where the youth is a victim rather than the perpetrator, as when charges of abuse or neglect are brought against a caretaker, an assessment of psychological trauma may be required. To be pertinent, a psychiatric consultation must address the specific issues that led to the consultation request.

For this reason, the psychiatrist must have an understanding of what these issues are so that he or she can be responsive. For while a psychiatrist should be expected to bring to any situation a concern and care for the individuals involved; an understanding of developmental psychology and family relationships; a capacity to assess, evaluate, and diagnose young people; and an overall professional integrity, all of this good will and competence may be to little avail if she or he does not bring it to bear on the issues at hand (2).

PHASES OF THE PROCESS: INTAKE

Intake Phase: Youth as Perpetrator

A review of Chapter 3 will indicate that the juvenile justice process can be roughly divided into the stages of intake, adjudication, and disposition. At intake, the responsible professionals must make the crucial decision about whether to forward the case for arraignment or to handle it informally (without court proceedings). In those cases in which the youth is the alleged perpetrator of a delinquent act, the youth must admit to the act before diversion can be considered. At this stage, the psychiatrist could be called in for a consultation in order to provide more information on the youth so that a more enlightened decision on diversion can be made. Either court-employed or private psychiatrists may be requested by an intake worker to perform an assessment for these purposes.

> Joseph, a 9-year-old boy, was referred to the court for the first time on a charge of public indecency after having exposed his genitals to a woman shopper. Due to the child's age and the nature of his offense, his probation officer requested a psychiatric consultation. He was accompanied by his aunt, who reported that both parents were long-time heroin addicts and had spent time in prison on drug charges. Different family members had taken care of the boy, and each had varying ideas about child development and discipline. By the age of 8 years, he was taking off from his elderly grandmother's home, staying out until midnight, stealing, and having behavioral difficulties at school. Through the department of children and youth services, he was hospitalized for 6 weeks on a psychiatric unit. He was diagnosed as having an attention-deficit disorder and was given a trial of methylphenidate hydrochloride (Ritalin), which markedly reduced his impulsivity and hyperactivity. Different types of counseling also began, which included parental guidance as well as individual work with the boy and monitoring of his behavior. Discharge recommendations, including continuing medication and counseling, were not followed by the family. His belligerent behavior necessitated transfer to a day program at a residential school nearby. After attending the school for 4 months, he was referred to the juvenile court. His aunt reported that he rarely was home,

stayed out all night, was being used by older boys to run drugs, and recently had sexually abused his 3-year-old cousin. The boy appeared disturbed during his interview, was restless and agitated, and exhibited few controls over his impulses. A therapeutic residential program was recommended urgently as the boy's behavior put him at considerable risk in his community.

Intake Phase: The Youth as Victim

An altogether different situation presents itself to the juvenile court when the child or adolescent is a victim rather than a perpetrator. Psychiatrists can find themselves asked to evaluate the degree to which a child or adolescent may have been damaged by suspected abuse on the part of the parents. They may also be asked to evaluate a parent from the standpoint of fitness to be a parent.

A particular concern for the psychiatrist doing such an evaluation is to avoid role confusion. The court evaluator should determine at the beginning of the assessment how much or how little reinvestigation of the original allegation should take place. This decision should depend on the quality of the past investigation as well as the referral questions from the court. The psychiatrist should take an active role in establishing the degree to which he or she will be involved in such a reinvestigation.

A fuller discussion of the psychiatrist's role in these matters may be found in Chapters 12, 13, and 16, which cover child abuse and termination of parental rights.

PHASES: ADJUDICATION

If a youth suspected of committing a delinquent act is not successfully diverted at the conclusion of the intake phase, the youngster will move on to the phase of adjudication. The first step in the adjudicative process is arraignment, as noted in Chapter 3. At this point, depending on the direction of the proceedings, the psychiatrist may be called in for a number of different purposes. Because adjudication is analogous to a trial in adult court, one issue that may arise concerns whether the juvenile is competent to undergo the proceeding.

Competency for Adjudication

Competency to stand trial in adult court has always been required as a precondition for trial. An individual who lacks the requisite understanding of the proceedings in which he or she is involved and the capacity to make decisions in his or her own best interest at the time of the trial is, in the eyes of the law, being tried in absentia. The criteria for competency in adult court as set down in the Supreme Court decision that dealt with the issue (*Dusky v. United States*) (3) are twofold: that the individual possess a rational and factual grasp of the charges and proceedings against him or her and that she or he be able to cooperate with the attorney in his or her own defense with a reasonable degree of rational understanding.

Should either or both of these conditions not apply by reason of mental illness or retardation, the adult defendant cannot be tried for these crimes until competency is restored. Another Supreme Court decision (*Jackson v. Indiana*) (4) makes it clear that although a person may be held involuntarily for purposes of treatment that might restore competency to the individual, he or she may not be held for this purpose beyond a reasonable period of time, usually considered to be a year. If at the end of a year an adult defendant has not yet returned to competency, the charges must be dropped and the individual freed (unless she or he remains hospitalized voluntarily or there are grounds for involuntary [civil] commitment).

As with other aspects of "due process" that were absent from the juvenile court until the decade of the 1960s, the requirement of competency as a condition for adjudication to take place was not applied during the first 70 years of the court's existence (1). Currently, however, a third of the states and the federal courts recognize this right and base the criteria for competency on the adult criminal law noted above.

Other states allow mental health examinations before adjudication and empower the court to commit a mentally ill youth for psychiatric treatment. Commitment for treatment usually is allowed only if the youth has been found to be mentally ill and dangerous to self or others by virtue of the illness.

Psychiatrist's Role in Determining Competency

Should the juvenile court feel that a child's competency is in question, it may appoint a psychiatrist to perform a competency evaluation. In this situation, the psychiatrist's usual examination must be supplemented by an inquiry into the effects of any mental illness on the youth's capacity to stand trial.

As of this writing, no Supreme Court decision has indicated that the criteria for competency in juveniles should be any different from those set forth in *Dusky v. United States* for adult defendants. Juvenile courts may utilize the *Dusky* criteria, may modify them, or may rely on their individual state statute.

Although the presence of a mental illness may raise the question of whether a youth is competent for trial, even a serious illness is not tantamount to a finding of incompetence. For such a finding to be made, the psychiatrist must address three questions: Does the youth have a factual grasp of the charges and proceedings against him or her? Does he or she also have a rational grasp of these charges and proceedings? Can he or she cooperate in the defense with a reasonable degree of rational understanding? Should the answer to any of these questions be "no," the youth should be considered incompetent.

Age, intelligence, school achievement, demeanor in contacts with attorneys, and prior court experience are all factors that an evaluating psychiatrist will incorporate in making a determination of competency. Table 5–1 indicates additional interview content that will assist the psychiatrist in answering the questions pertinent to a finding of competency.

> Edgar, a 15-year-old boy, was charged with several offenses including criminal trespass, burglary, larceny, and threatening. Two months after these referrals were made, he was charged with a serious juvenile offense, assault in the first degree. At that time, his oldest sister noted strange behavior and called the police. He was immediately hospitalized on a 15-day emergency certificate to an adolescent psychiatric ward. His symptoms included hearing voices and bizarre behavior, i.e., shaving off his eyebrows, slashing his face and chest with a knife, and threatening his mother with a machete after destroying household property. On admission, he was found to be actively psychotic, delusional, and hallucinating. During the hospitalization, he was treated with a drug to reduce his agitation, but his condition remained unchanged. The family wanted him home, and the boy was discharged against medical advice after his 15-day period was up. Several weeks later at his arraignment in court, a psychiatric evaluation was ordered to assess his psychological state and whether the court should proceed with the matter. The psychiatrist found that Edgar was actively psychotic and that this condition prevented him from being able to work with the public defender. The psychiatrist recommended that Edgar be returned to the hospital by court order for further treatment.

If the psychiatrist is retained to testify at a competency hearing, or if a written report is required, the psychiatrist must be prepared to explain how the mental illness has rendered the youth incompetent.

Competency is ultimately a legal rather than a medical determination, and the final decision as to competency is therefore made by the judge. Should he or she find the youth incompetent, the judge will generally commit the youth for treatment, either inpatient or outpatient. In some states, a finding of incompetency will result in dismissal of the charges, and treatment becomes the final disposition. In many others, the courts do not relinquish jurisdiction automatically; only if the juvenile cannot be returned to competency in a "reasonable" period of time will the charges be dropped.

Because of this, the competency hearing may be the last judicial involvement that a mentally ill juvenile has with these charges. It is important to keep in mind, at least with older adolescents, that this situation may create an incentive to avoid further court involvement by feigning mental illness. For this reason, a psychiatrist may be well advised to maintain a certain index of suspicion and keep in mind that he or she might be a potential target for manipulation by some youths.

Table 5–1.   Development of a children's competency assessment interview: current status

---

- Understanding of charges
  Why one has been brought to juvenile court
  What one is being accused of
  One's perceptions of the degree of seriousness of the accusation, and others' probable perceptions of its seriousness

- Understanding of matters essential to cooperation with one's lawyer
  Recognition that one has a lawyer
  Knowledge of the lawyer's name
  The idea that the lawyer is on one's side
  Appropriate appreciation of that which the lawyer will endeavor to do
  What one could tell the lawyer that would be relevant to the lawyer's intention to help

- Understanding of court proceedings and personnel
  What generally will happen in court
  Approximate locations (in courtroom) and functional labels for various key personnel
  Judge's role
  Jury's role (if relevant)
  Definition of a witness
  Definition of evidence
  Definition of district attorney or prosecutor
  One's role and expected behavior in the courtroom
  Appropriate response to evidence that contradicts one's own information or point of view

- Understanding of consequences
  Meaning of "guilt" and "innocence"
  What will happen if the court concludes either
  One's feelings about the various possible consequences

Source.   Reprinted with permission of Michael D. Stein, Bonnie L. Padrusch, and Carol Goldberg.

Transfer or Waiver

Certain psychiatric evaluations will be requested because the court is considering transferring or waiving older (or even middle) adolescents to adult court because of the seriousness of their alleged crimes. If convicted in adult court, youthful offenders are exposed to the possibility of sentences far lengthier than the maximum that can be imposed in juvenile court or, in extreme cases, even the death penalty.

To make such weighty decisions, the court must concern itself primarily with the offender's likely future behavior: that is, whether he or she displays real potential for rehabilitation, perhaps through treatment. If the answer to this question is "yes," the court will most likely continue its own jurisdiction over the offender, in keeping with its role. If the answer is "no," the alleged offender is more likely to be transferred to the adult system. Obviously, a psychiatric evaluation can be central to the court's determination in this area.

> For example, three juveniles are examined who have committed murders. In the first case, a psychiatrist finds that the youth is mentally ill. In the second, the doctor discovers that the murdered person had been abusing the youth sexually for years. In a third, the murder is accidental and occurs while the youth is intoxicated. In all three cases, the psychiatrist might recommend retaining the youths in juvenile court because of the circumstances of the crimes and the likelihood that treatment in each case would lead to the rehabilitation of these offenders.

If a youthful offender is not transferred out of juvenile court and has not been previously diverted, the adjudication phase will begin.

CRIMINAL RESPONSIBILITY: THE INSANITY DEFENSE

In the trial phase of adult court the services of a forensic psychiatrist are often sought in connection with the insanity defense. This defense, when successful, results in a finding of NGBRI, a special form of acquittal, and ordinarily leads to commitment at a public mental hospital until the person is no longer mentally ill or dangerous.

Insanity is a legal term applied to individuals who are held to be not responsible for their crimes because of a mental illness at the time the crime was committed. Whether or not a mentally ill person is found to be insane and therefore not responsible depends on whether that person is believed to have acted intentionally or with a "guilty" mind to commit the crime. Only if the mental illness is so severe that it is found to have prevented the individual from forming the intent to commit the crime can it form a basis for a successful insanity plea.

A psychotic man sees the Devil in a shop window and throws a rock through it. He is arrested and charged with destruction of property. At his trial he is found NGBRI on the charges because the court believes 1) that he was suffering from a major mental illness at the time of the crime and 2) that because of it he was unable to form the intent to destroy the shop owner's property.

In juvenile court, the insanity defense has made a fairly recent appearance, because for many years it was considered not only unnecessary but logically inconsistent as well. An adjudication of delinquency was not considered to be a criminal conviction; therefore, there was no criminal responsibility from which the delinquent need be exempted.

In the late 1960s and 1970s, however, as the Supreme Court introduced more and more due process protections to juvenile proceedings, the insanity defense began to be discussed as a possibly necessary element (5). A few states have recognized the right to put forth an insanity defense in juvenile cases. Even in adult court, the insanity defense is less often used and very much less often successful than the general public tends to believe. As uncommon as it is in adult court, it is far more uncommon in juvenile court. In spite of this, the psychiatrist practicing in a jurisdiction where the insanity defense for juveniles exists may be called on to perform such an evaluation.

How does the court decide whether a defendant was so mentally ill at the time of the crime that the youth lacked the intent to commit it? Different jurisdictions use different criteria to make this determination. Some jurisdictions have modeled their statutes after the American Law Institute's Model Penal Code (see Glossary). This document sets out two criteria, one "cognitive" and one "volitional." The cognitive prong of the insanity defense has to do with whether the individual, by virtue of mental illness, was unable at the time of the crime to "appreciate the wrongfulness of his acts." The volitional prong is usually stated in terms of whether the individual, by virtue of a mental illness, was "unable to conform his behavior to the requirements of the law." If either or both of these criteria are met, the individual is considered to have been unable to form the intent necessary for conviction and is acquitted by reason of insanity.

Some states have only a cognitive rule in effect, as does the federal statute. Others have gone back to an earlier formulation known as the M'Naughten rule, which states that an NGBRI finding may occur only if, at the time of the crime and by virtue of a mental illness, that person did not know what he or she was doing, or if that person did know, then he or she did not know that it was wrong.

Any psychiatrist who is invited to perform an insanity evaluation must be aware of the precise criteria in use in his or her state. Whatever officer of the court has contacted the psychiatrist to perform such an evaluation can act as a resource for such information. The psychiatrist should not feel inhibited about querying these individuals at length and even meeting with them so that the evaluator can be quite clear on the questions that she or he is being asked to address.

Table 5–2 compares certain aspects of the insanity defense evaluation with aspects of the evaluations for competency for adjudication and for transfer to adult court. For example, the insanity evaluation concerns itself with a previous mental state, the mental state at the time of the crime, whereas the competency examination is a "present state" evaluation, concerned with the current mental functioning of the person. By contrast, the transfer evaluation is concerned primarily with what can be inferred or predicted about the individual's future functioning. In the same way, the criteria for findings of insanity, competency, and waiver to adult court are briefly summarized.

PHASES: DISPOSITION

Once a youth is adjudicated a delinquent, a disposition must be found for him or her. The dispositional phase of the process is thus analogous to the sentencing that goes on after a finding of guilt in the adult court. It is at

Table 5–2.   Comparison of evaluation criteria for selected forensic issues in juvenile court

	Insanity defense	Competency	Transfer
Time frame	Time of crime (past)	Time of evaluation (present)	Prognosis (future)
Criteria	Capacity to form intent	Capacity to help defend self	Potential for rehabilitation
Controlling court cases	State and federal statutes	*Dusky v. U.S.*	*Kent v. U.S.* and statutes
Outcomes	NGBRI vs. adjudication	Incompetent for adjudication vs. competent	Waived to adult court vs. adjudicated in juvenile court
Disposition	Mental hospital vs. disposition	Treatment to restore competency vs. cleared for adjudication	Tried in adult court vs. adjudicated in juvenile court

Note.   NGBRI = not guilty by reason of insanity.

disposition that courts most commonly call on psychiatrists for assistance. At this stage, questions of prognosis, amenability to treatment, and the type of treatment indicated, including whether a secure facility is desirable, are of the greatest concern to the court as it attempts to individualize a plan for the youthful offender.

One decision that must sometimes be made is whether an offender should be allowed to remain in the community and, if so, whether the youth should continue to live at home. For example, if an older brother has committed a sexual offense against a younger sister, such a recommendation, if made, is likely to be rejected.

The examining psychiatrist will need to learn more about the home before issuing a recommendation one way or the other. Under such circumstances, the doctor should incorporate an assessment of the parents and other members of the household as appropriate into the overall evaluation of the situation.

Adolescence is a time in which the young person undergoes a process of separation and individuation from his or her parents. At the outset of this phase, the youth will be deeply involved in the family structure, but by its conclusion he or she should be functioning relatively independently of it. For this reason, delinquent behavior, no less than other forms of behavioral disturbance, may represent the workings of a disturbed family dynamic when the offenders are chronologically or psychologically in early adolescence. Since Johnson and Szurek's classic work in 1952 (6), for example, it has been observed that juveniles may act out antisocial impulses of their parents that are covertly transmitted and even subtly rewarded. In other cases, young people have been known to commit crimes in order to focus attention on problems in their families—a cry for help (7).

If such is the case, the extent and nature of the family pathology will become evident only when the family as well as the offender is assessed. Under such circumstances it may be the wisest disposition to keep the youth in the community and have at least a portion of the treatment take place in a family context.

Ultimately, most teenagers separate psychologically from their parents. Thereafter, the parents are no longer a significant daily influence in their lives. Once such a point is reached, treatment for the parents or in a family setting may be less fruitful for the youth. Many disturbed youths are found to have separated prematurely from their parents, usually as a result of having grown up with grossly abusive and neglectful parental figures. Such youths are typically victims of or witnesses to verbal, physical, and sexual abuse. They will never have experienced the nurturing environment that normal development requires. Such teenagers will have concluded that no one other than themselves can be trusted and that the wisest course is to avoid forming relationships in which one can be hurt again. Anyone indicating that he or she cares for the teenager will be met with suspicion and disbelief (8).

In cases of this sort the best interests of the youth may require placement in residential treatment away from the influence of such destructive parental figures. The presence of healthier, more caring role models and a more therapeutic environment may help to tempt youths out of the isolation into which they have locked themselves in desperate attempts to avoid the further pain of further connection with such parents.

As is noted in much greater detail in Chapter 9, the psychiatrist must not only develop and present a professional understanding of the offender, he or she must also be aware of the resources available to the courts for rendering the appropriate treatment, if treatment is recommended.

Different jurisdictions have widely differing sets of options available to the court. Sometimes the matter is money: wealthy jurisdictions will have better public services and, on occasion, the financial resources to send certain youngsters to private residential facilities. On other occasions, location is the problem: jurisdictions nearer population centers may have a wider range of treatment facilities than more rural ones. Sometimes the youth's family resources may make the difference between a public and a private facility.

SPECIAL ISSUES

Six special issues are discussed later in this handbook. They are drug abuse, physical abuse, sexual abuse, juvenile sex offenders, violent juveniles, and termination of parental rights. In the late 1980s all of these issues emerged into prominence because of the apparent dramatic increase in the incidence of these problems. To a great degree, the question of termination of parental rights has become more commonly considered as a result of the increase in substance abuse, physical abuse, and sexual abuse by parents. Especially tragic are cases in which the parent or parents are themselves juveniles who have never been adequately parented and display little concern for or tolerance of their often-accidental children.

In some of these cases, the psychiatrist involved in disposition planning must be prepared to think about not one or two generations but three and sometimes four. The doctor must expect to encounter unique examples of what is meant by a "home." He or she may be forced to weigh what appear to be unsatisfactory alternatives in order to find the one that is the least unsatisfactory for the child before the court. Such are the challenges that exist behind the doors of the juvenile court.

REFERENCES

1. Grisso T, Miller MO, Sales B: Competency to stand trial in juvenile court. Int J Law Psychiatry 10:1–20, 1987
2. Slovenko R: Psychiatry and the Law. Boston, MA, Little, Brown, 1973, pp 18–38
3. Dusky v United States, 362 US 402, 1960
4. Jackson v Indiana, 406 US 715, 92 SCt 1845, 32 L.Ed.2d 435, 1972
5. Harrington MM, Keary AO: The insanity defense in juvenile delinquency proceedings. Bull Am Acad Psychiatry Law 8(3):272–279, 1980
6. Johnson AM, Szurek SA: The genesis of antisocial acting out in children and adults. Psychoanal Q 21:323–332, 1952
7. Blos P: The second individuation process of adolescence. Psychoanal Study Child 22:162–186, 1967
8. Marohn R: Hospital treatment of the behaviorally disordered adolescent, in The Treatment of Antisocial Syndromes. Edited by Reid W. New York, Van Nostrand Reinhold, 1981, pp 146–161

CHAPTER 6

THE CLINICAL EVALUATION
FOR JUVENILE COURT

Kathleen M. Quinn, M.D.

The impact of the clinical evaluation in juvenile court is both different and potentially more serious than other clinical encounters. For the youth, the evaluation may lead to a loss of freedom in a juvenile justice facility. For society, the evaluation may address who is treatable and who is not, as well as who is more likely to be a recidivist and who is not. The evaluator may address multiple issues including diagnosis; the impact of biology, society, and family issues on the youth; and the dynamic significance and meaning of the youth's behavior. The evaluator will also encounter a wide range of ages among the people evaluated, including the very young in abuse, neglect, or custody cases; older adolescents who are facing unruly or delinquent complaints; and parents or interested parties in all cases. Each evaluator should consider the limitations of his or her training, interest, and comfort in assessing various age groups. In addition, clinical administrators should maintain a balance in staff to permit appropriate assignments of cases to qualified individuals.

The psychiatrist conducting a clinical evaluation for juvenile court should approach the task as an investigation. The evaluation should be performed by someone other than the mental health professional who has had an ongoing therapeutic relationship with the child and/or family. This separation of roles overcomes problems of bias, confidentiality, and maintenance of the patient-therapist alliance. Multiple countertransference issues may be encountered by the court evaluator. Feelings of anger, fear, disgust, or hopelessness may confront the clinician and need to be addressed.

Psychiatrists performing these evaluations must set aside the assumption that individuals they interview are always telling them the truth. Traditional clinical practice has usually assumed the veracity of patients when describing their history and their symptoms. However, in all forensic settings, including juvenile court, this assumption is naive. Assessment of an individual's honesty and accuracy may be crucial in the juvenile

37

court, especially when the clinician is asked to evaluate the treatability of an individual or a family. The clinical assessment of the consistency, accuracy, and completeness of the individual's self-report compared with the collateral sources and documents is best done by a mental health professional who does not have an ongoing therapeutic relationship with the child and/or family. The forensic clinician, however, must also remain aware that the judge, not the clinician, is the ultimate fact finder.

To be an effective witness, the evaluator must be willing to spend sufficient time to gather and to analyze large amounts of information. The evaluator should also have the skills to communicate this opinion in a clear, concise manner to the court, both in writing and verbally, in testimony. (See Chapter 8.) Before accepting a case, the psychiatrist must be assured by the referring attorney or agency that he or she will be permitted to interview all persons relevant to the matter before the court and be given access to relevant collateral data such as school, medical, agency, and mental health records. The negotiation of the scope of the evaluation, method of payment, and time line of evaluation are critical steps before accepting the case. If the psychiatrist is unfamiliar with the standard pertaining to the pending legal issue, she or he should request a copy of the relevant statute and/or case law and consider seeking consultation from a colleague experienced in juvenile justice matters before initiating the evaluation. A clinician employed by the court may be limited in the time and scope of the evaluation by financial and caseload restraints. Still, the psychiatrist must decide what is necessary for the evaluation in order to form an opinion with reasonable medical certainty.

The format of the evaluations differs depending on the issue before the court. However, several clinical issues are commonly encountered in juvenile court. Most youngsters facing delinquency or unruly complaints would rather appear "bad" than "mad." The interviewer must be willing to explore beyond the defensiveness to determine if the mental status examination or history suggests disorders other than conduct disorder pathology. Denial of the allegations is also frequently encountered. Adequate collateral sources, such as victim statements or mental health records, may permit confrontation of the denial concerning the current offense or psychiatric symptoms. A careful review of past antisocial acts may permit an assessment of a pattern of conduct-disordered behaviors even in the face of denial concerning the current complaint.

Care must be taken before assuming that denial is conscious lying and another example of antisocial behavior. Individuals in juvenile court (including adolescents interviewed during waiver proceedings) are often interviewed in the preadjudicatory phase of the proceedings. Denial at this phase is often appropriately self-serving and legally prudent. Clinical assessment of the amount of denial is more appropriate to the postadjudicatory phase of the proceedings. Occasionally, classical malingering may be encountered in juvenile court. In such cases, older adolescents may exaggerate or falsely produce symptoms in order to gain transfer to a civil hospital from a detention center.

Beneath the "tough" exterior also may be significant depression or other serious psychopathology. The evaluator often must take the time and care to probe for these less acceptable feelings and symptoms in this population.

Each individual interviewed for the assessment must be given a clear explanation of the role of the evaluator, the purpose of the evaluation, and its lack of confidentiality. The individuals being interviewed or the appropriate guardian should be asked to sign necessary release forms to gather collateral data.

DELINQUENCY AND STATUS OFFENSE EVALUATIONS

The ultimate purpose of these evaluations is to describe to the court the youth's past and present functioning, the level of individual and family psychopathology, and treatment needs. Court records, probation reports, and other documents should be reviewed before beginning the clinical interviews. In order to maximize information gathering, the initial portion of the interview should be spent attempting to establish some rapport with the youngster. This may be accomplished, for example, by discussing his or her reactions to being held in a detention or shelter-care facility. Such an exchange may also permit the evaluator an opportunity to note the youth's verbal abilities and apparent intellectual endowment so the rest of the interview may be appropriately tailored to the youngster's level.

> A child psychiatry fellow failed to appreciate that a 17-year-old sex offender's suave verbal style masked low borderline intellectual functioning and considerable social deprivation. The fellow became increasingly frustrated when he attempted to gather a sexual history using words such as "ejaculation" and "masturbation." The fellow attributed the youth's lack of responses to denial and defensiveness. However, the supervisor was able to conduct a second interview with the adolescent using more appropriate language that yielded considerably more clinical data concerning the youth's sexual life.

The youth should be asked to describe his or her current living situation, daily activities, and contact with professionals. Inquiry should be made concerning any medical illnesses or substance use. Current stresses or concerns affecting the child and family should be discussed.

Relevant past history should be explored with an emphasis on the quality of relationships, level of supervision, and nature of limit setting within the family. Important losses or separations should be detailed. The family's involvement with protective service agencies should be noted. The child's and family's history of use of psychiatric services and substance use should be recorded. Emphasis should be placed on gathering data relevant to treatable conditions such as attention-deficit disorder, mood or thought disorders, or specific developmental disorders. The child's educational history should also be reviewed, with particular emphasis on history related to specific learning problems and the impact of the child's behavior on learning. The youngster's likes or dislikes with respect to subjects and teachers may permit a beginning assessment of academic strengths and weaknesses, as well as the quality of relationships with adults outside the family.

A detailed review should be made of the child's history of antisocial activities (e.g., fire setting, truancy, runaway behaviors, history of fights, use of weapons, cruelty to animals or people, gang involvement, thefts, vandalism). The evaluator can increase the data gathering by prefacing this portion of the interview with the statement that the questions concern behaviors that many youngsters who come before the juvenile court have experienced. The evaluator should attempt to understand any patterns or precipitants of the child's behaviors. The youngster should be questioned about experiencing any form of physical or sexual maltreatment. Patterns of peer relationships, hobbies or interests, and aspirations should also be discussed.

> An adolescent before the court on a truancy complaint described an intense involvement with Satanic worship. His room was decorated with occult symbols. His close peers were all involved in the rituals. Exploration on mental status examination revealed numerous characteristics of a developing schizotypal personality. This level of psychopathology caused the court clinician to make specific recommendations for psychiatric follow-up and special educational services for this youth.

All youngsters should receive a detailed mental status examination. Lewis (1) recommends a nonthreatening manner of inquiring about hallucinatory events that includes questions such as "Have your eyes (ears, etc.) played tricks on you?" and "What was that like?" These questions may be embedded in the medical screening questions. Questions concerning depersonalization, derealization, déjà vu, suspiciousness, and episodes of amnesia while not using substances should also be included, in addition to the standard questions concerning mood and thought processes. Such questions serve as screening questions. The intellectual portion of the mental status examination should be left until the end of the interview because it is often threatening to these youngsters, who frequently have long histories of academic failure.

The use of psychological testing and neurological consultation should be tailored to each child's history and symptoms. Considerable redundancy in assessment can be avoided by reviewing past evaluations for content and results. A screening of intellectual functioning (e.g., Wechsler Intelligence Scale for Children, short form [2]) and a personality instrument (e.g., Minnesota Multiphasic Personality Inventory [3] or Jesness Inventory [4]) may be sufficient in uncomplicated cases where no testing has been performed previously. Services from a school or a head injury clinic outside the court may need to be sought to complete full psychoeducational or neuropsychological batteries. These specialized batteries may be imperative in tailoring a specific treatment program.

> A 16-year-old adolescent before the court on seven complaints of breaking and entering had a history of severe head trauma 1 year before while making a getaway in a stolen car. His history revealed many episodes of breaking and entering. However, since the accident, he demonstrated numerous symptoms of dementia with a loss of intellectual functioning and behavioral disinhibition. His stealing had continued, but he was now less successful at avoiding detection. He and his family had failed to follow through with a rehabilitation program with a local head injury clinic. The court was informed of this history and permitted a closely supervised outpatient resumption of his assessment and rehabilitation services through the head trauma clinic rather than automatic commitment to a state juvenile justice facility without such specialized services.

Whenever possible, the parents of the youngster before the court should be seen. This interview has several purposes: 1) providing history to supplement or corroborate the juvenile's own account, 2) evaluating family functioning and its possible contribution to the causes of the delinquent behavior, 3) assessing the need of the family or an individual parent for services, and 4) deciding how helpful the family can be in carrying out recommendations.

> A 15-year-old girl was before the court on a complaint of domestic violence. Both the girl and her mother had explosive tempers. When interviewed, the mother acknowledged a history of losing control that dated back to this girl's infancy, including a range of behaviors from throwing the girl when she was much younger to taking a board to her in recent weeks. Immediate separation of the pair was recommended, because there was no evidence that either the mother or daughter could disengage from these violent confrontations.

Throughout the evaluation, the clinician should be seeking clues to the youth's treatability, both in mental health treatment facilities and in other services and sites available through the court. The degree of anxiety and conflict about acting-out behaviors, motivation, verbal skills, and capacity to accept clarification and interpretation may permit the clinician to address the adolescent's ability to work in traditional modalities. The search for both vulnerabilities and strengths during the evaluation should permit the clinician to propose an integrated treatment plan.

ABUSE AND NEGLECT CASES

The issues before the court on abuse and neglect cases often include the treatability of the parent(s), the feasibility of reuniting the family unit, and/or the service needs of the affected child or children. Each question may require a different form of interview(s). The treatability of the parent(s) may be addressed in an individual assessment of parenting capacity, including each parent's capacity for empathy, ability to provide reasonable consistency and limit setting, ability to be nurturing, ability to care for basic family needs, and capacity to utilize services offered to improve parenting skills. The interview(s) should include extensive review of the parents' own experience of being parented, their knowledge of the developmental needs of their children, and their current appreciation of their strengths and deficits as parents. They should be asked how they would respond to various common parenting dilemmas such as the management of a sick child, disciplining a child, or management of a tantrum. A review of the stresses and any psychiatric disorders that impaired their parenting in the past should also be made.

Beginning the parental interviews with the parent's own history may permit establishment of rapport before discussing the abuse and neglect issues before the court. Clinical research indicates a better prognosis for those abusive parents who can recognize their own childhood experiences of abuse and who make a conscious effort to act differently toward their children. Parents should be asked to describe in detail the types of punishments they experienced and their current assessment of these acts. Detailed history gathering may yield considerable data even from parents attempting to put their best foot forward.

> One mother was asked to review her different residences during the year that her two children had been in placement. She detailed multiple moves and evictions, including her return the day before the interview to a shelter for women.

> Another mother described a 6-year history of cocaine and amphetamine abuse that she stated had stopped 2 years before. However, she described current daily marijuana and alcohol use that had begun after her stimulant use had stopped. She was in no substance abuse treatment program and did not see a reason to pursue treatment because she believed that her drug problem was over.

A full family assessment should be conducted when the issue of reunification or parental termination is present (see Chapter 16). Such an evaluation includes individual, parental, and child interviews, as well as observations of the parent and child(ren) together. The evaluator should seek to understand the quality and intensity of the child's attachment to the biological parent(s) and the child's perception of the parent's functioning. In addition, the special needs of both child and parent should be evaluated, including the natural parents' ability to provide for these needs.

Data concerning attachment behaviors may be gathered through play, interactional observations, drawing, and informal contact (such as in the waiting area).

> Two children who had not lived with their mother since infancy sat together on one chair and interacted with each other, ignoring their biological mother with whom they had not visited for over a year. Neither child (ages 7 and 5 years) had any understanding of who she was. Both identified their long-term foster parents as "mommy" and "daddy" and spoke frequently of their activities together in the foster family when interviewed alone.

> A 4-year-old boy drew his foster family, his biological aunt and uncle, and his siblings in his family drawing. He also added his biological mother, whom he then scribbled out, saying that she was mean. He appeared overtly frightened as he described the physical abuse he had experienced at her hands. He refused to see her even with considerable support from the evaluator and his social worker.

Evaluators should seek to describe patterns of observations to support their conclusions. Direct quotes may be especially helpful in supporting the conclusions. The individual interviews with the children should not be an attempt to reinvestigate the alleged abuse or neglect, a task that will have been accomplished by protective service agencies and/or the police. Rather, the individual child interviews should be designed to assess the child's psychological ties and psychological functioning.

> A 6-year-old girl appeared sad and apathetic in her individual interview, an observation confirmed by her foster parents and social worker. Her family drawing consisted of only herself. She described frequent episodes of anger directed at herself with intermittent suicidal ideation. Her biological mother had noted similar symptoms in the past but obtained no services for her. On observation with her mother, the child was withdrawn and began to talk in baby talk. Her foster parents described other symptoms consistent with posttraumatic stress disorder secondary to severe neglect and physical abuse, which was well documented by collateral data. The data from this evaluation were used to get immediate mental health services for this child.

Personality testing (e.g., Minnesota Multiphasic Personality Inventory [3] and Millon Adolescent Personality Inventory [5]) may be helpful in supporting clinical observations and history. Evidence of significant characterological deficits on testing may be relevant to the issue of treatability if they are supported by other clinical data. Intellectual testing is appropriate with parents who have clear intellectual deficits. Occasionally, a child will be tested due to an identified or suspected disorder, most often learning or intellectual deficits.

Clinicians should not infer that a diagnosis of a mental disorder makes a parent unfit. The relevant question must always be what impact any mental disorder has on the individual's capacity to parent adequately and to respond to interventions.

COMPETENCY TO STAND TRIAL

As described in Chapter 5, almost all jurisdictions use the definition of the Supreme Court in *Dusky v. United States* (6) as the standard by which evaluations of competency to stand trial should be performed. The clinical examination of the juvenile should attempt to assess *1)* the juvenile's understanding of the legal complaint(s), *2)* the juvenile's capacity to cooperate with his or her lawyer, *3)* the juvenile's understanding of court proceedings and the functions of court personnel, and *4)* the juvenile's understanding of the possible outcomes of the legal proceedings. In addition, the evaluation should describe the presence or absence of a mental disorder or intellectual deficit and its impact on each of these functions. Many states specify that the deficits must be due to a mental disorder in order to qualify the juvenile as incompetent to stand trial.

Previous research may be relevant to assessing competency. For example, contrary to judicial and clinical assumption, prior court experience may not be a good indication of the juvenile's degree of knowledge about the court (7). White juveniles demonstrated increased knowledge about the court, well above the mean for a juvenile court sample, but only with prior arrests. The inverse was found for black juveniles.

If a question remains concerning the capacity of the juvenile to relate to counsel, the clinician may choose to call the attorney to obtain direct information concerning the attorney-juvenile interaction. Several excellent semistructured interview protocols exist, but they were developed for assessing an adult defendant's knowledge of and capacity to relate to criminal court proceedings. The clinician must be aware of both the procedural differences between criminal and juvenile court and the appropriate language in which to phrase relevant questions.

A 16-year-old adolescent already in placement was facing a complaint of grand theft. His IQ was 63 and he had no sign of a major mental illness. His major deficits relevant to competency to stand trial included his lack of knowledge of courtroom proceedings and personnel. The forensic evaluator submitted a report recommending a finding of incompetency based on this evaluation. The report recommended that the teen could be restored to competence by an educational program coordinated by his special education teacher at his secure residential center and the coordinator of a local adult forensic unit.

REFERENCES

1. Lewis DO: Diagnostic evaluation of the delinquent child: psychiatric, psychological, neurological, and educational components, in Child Psychiatry and the Law. Edited by Schetky DH, Benedek EP. New York, Brunner/Mazel, 1980, pp 139–155
2. Wechsler D: Wechsler Intelligence Scale for Children, Revised. San Antonio, TX, Psychological Corporation, 1974
3. Hathaway SR, McKinley JC: Minnesota Multiphasic Personality Inventory—2. Minneapolis, University of Minnesota, 1989
4. Jesness CA: The Jesness Inventory Manual. Palo Alto, CA, Consulting Psychologists Press, 1983
5. Millon T, Green CJ, Meagher RB Jr: Millon Adolescent Personality Inventory. Minneapolis, MN, NCS Interpretive Scoring System, 1976–82
6. Dusky v United States, 362 US 402, 1960
7. Grisso T: Juveniles' Waiver of Rights: Legal and Psychological Competence. New York, Plenum, 1981

CHAPTER 7

THE PSYCHIATRIC REPORT IN THE JUVENILE JUSTICE SYSTEM

Carl P. Malmquist, M.D., M.S.

The psychiatric report for use in a juvenile court proceeding is the most important document a psychiatrist working in the juvenile justice system can produce. Well-reasoned, clinical conclusions can have a significant impact on the proceedings. After examining the youngster and his or her family, the psychiatrist must cull from the sometimes extensive information gathered those facts and impressions that are most pertinent to the court's concerns. One must organize these facts and impressions in a logical, orderly fashion (facts first, impressions later), present them clearly and intelligibly (remembering that one is writing for laypersons), and support impressions and conclusions competently and convincingly. The report is a summary of the relevant findings of the evaluation, the conclusions that the clinician is able to draw, the recommendations, and a discussion of the rationale for the recommendations. A good report reflects the psychiatrist's keen awareness of the nature and limits of his or her expertise, sticks to the mental health issues, and is authoritative without being arrogant. Positive findings are what concern the court; long lists of negatives tend to be boring and distracting. In general, succinctness is highly desirable, perhaps no more than 5 to 10 pages. Lengthy reports encourage busy judges to skim, possibly missing important passages in the body of the report. It is advisable that the most important arguments be recapitulated and highlighted in the summary and closing discussion. It is unfortunate but true that too often only the final paragraphs of the report get read.

Some matters essential to the writing of a competent report will have been dealt with at the time of the evaluation or earlier. A clear delineation of what the court or the lawyer requesting the evaluation is looking for is paramount. Some of the questions raised at the point of referral may not be appropriate or fall within the expertise of the psychiatrist. This issue should be dealt with at the time of referral. Second, the psychiatrist will have decided how to elucidate the mental health issues in the case and will have conducted the evaluation accordingly. Last, some thought will have been given already to how the examination might cast some light on the legal questions before the court. Any uncertainty on the clinician's part should have been clarified in discussions with the lawyers, probation officer, or even the judge before the examination.

At the time of the examination, the youth and his or her family will have been advised that a report will be written to the court after the evaluation procedure and that anything arising in the course of the interview might well be included in that report (the confidentiality warning). Although juvenile court proceedings are protected from the public, there is always a possibility that a psychiatric report will be read beyond the confines of the juvenile court proceedings (e.g., at treatment facilities receiving referred materials from the court). Discretion that protects the privacy of third parties must always be exercised.

The report must be written with the understanding that its author may be called into court to defend it. This includes cross-examination in an adversarial context. Although by all indications mental health examiners are very infrequently called on to testify in juvenile court, they must always be prepared to do so. A good report anticipates the questions that may be raised by opposing lawyers or the judge and attempts to deal with them as sensitively and thoroughly as possible. A thoughtful, well-written report minimizes the chance that a subsequent appearance in court will be an uncomfortable or embarrassing experience for the clinician. As in all such situations, inclusion of irrelevant or extraneous material in the report merely increases the risk that a witness will be led into awkward, unconvincing testimony.

The psychiatric report is a permanent record of what the clinician has to say. As such, it is as much a statement about the clinician's abilities and competence as it is of the substantive issues in the case. Reputations are built or may fall on the quality of such reports. Maintaining a high level of performance does credit to the individual clinician and increases respect for the profession as a whole. Outside of juvenile court (e.g., in domestic relations court on a custody matter, where the proceedings, unless sealed, are in the public domain), parts of a psychiatric report may be quoted in the media and its author named.

The importance of writing style cannot be overstated. A simple, direct style that rigorously avoids jargon or esoteric language is essential. Psychiatric concepts that should be included must either be quite understandable to lawyers and other non-mental-health professionals or else clearly explained. Generally speaking, and in contrast to the standard psychiatric evaluation written in a psychiatric hospital or clinic setting, a report to the court is descriptive, emphasizing behavior rather than unconscious processes, and avoids complex psychoanalytic theorizing, however relevant that may appear to the clinician. This is not to say that there is no place for elucidation of psychodynamic issues. On the contrary, in a given case they may be the most important ideas the psychiatrist can contribute, whether they concern either individual or family dynamics.

The more skillfully drafted a report is, the more likely it is to receive a favorable reception by the court. Table 7–1 provides an outline for use when constructing a psychiatric report. The major practical benefit is that dispositional recommendations made in the report will be supported and hopefully implemented. In this way, the psychiatrist can become a powerful advocate promoting the best interests of the child, at least as seen from the mental health perspective.

OUTLINE OF THE REPORT

Every report consists of two general components: *1)* standard elements contained in all reports and *2)* elements specific to the particular case. The outline that follows must be modified accordingly to suit the requirements of the case at hand. One general recommendation is to distinguish sharply

---

Table 7–1.   Outline of the content of a psychiatric report

I. Introductory section
    A. Identifying information
    B. Reason for referral
    C. Sources of information
II. The examination
    A. History of current problems(s)
    B. Past personal history
        1. Family history
        2. School history
        3. Personal and social histories
        4. Substance abuse history
        5. Developmental and medical history
        6. Psychiatric history
        7. Legal history
    C. Mental status examination
    D. Psychological testing
    E . Interviews with family
III. Diagnostic formulation
IV. Summary of psychiatric findings and discussion of legal questions and recommendations

between the "fact" portion of the report and the "opinion" part. Mixing the two is confusing at best. At worst, it may subject the entire report to undue criticism.

CONTENTS OF THE REPORT

I. Introductory Section

A. Identifying Information

This information includes name, birth date, file number (if any), and date that the juvenile and others were seen, whether singly or jointly, for how long, and where. The patient's condition at the time of the examination, i.e., whether the patient was alert, oriented, and cooperative or seemingly under the influence of drugs or alcohol, should be noted and any impact on the examination should be mentioned. The same applies if the juvenile's contact with reality was impaired, limiting the effectiveness of the interview. If the patient seemed to be drugged, was this due to prescribed medication?

It should also be noted if a confidentiality warning (see Chapter 6) was given and to whom.

B. Reason for Referral

The referral source, whether the court, a lawyer, or the family; the reason for the request; and the legal questions before the court should be noted. Possible reasons for referral include consideration of waiver (transfer) to adult court, suspicion of mental illness or defect, a request for evaluation of treatment needs and treatability, transfer to a psychiatric hospital, assessment of dangerousness, and competency. With respect to the juvenile's personality, the court may also be interested in his or her credibility as a witness. This would be particularly important in a child abuse case, for example.

C. Sources of Information

These include all documents forwarded to the examiner by the court, probation officer, or lawyers; any additional documents such as hospital records, school or work records, or social services materials that may be solicited by the examiner; psychological reports; and all other materials read. In addition, all telephone contacts should be listed. Occasionally, police records may be relevant and contribute to the picture.

II. The Examination

The time actually spent in interviewing the juvenile and his or her parents generally produces the most valuable material to be included in the report. It is in the interviews that most of the questions raised by the court are likely to be answered. Making these points stand out clearly in this part of the report will facilitate subsequent discussion and tying together of the main points to be made in the summation.

Important variations in the way a report is written will stem from the differences in the types of cases before the court. Thus the major emphasis in a juvenile delinquency matter will be on the examination of the juvenile, although much may be gained by seeing the parents as well. In an abuse or neglect situation, examination of the parents is more critical, and the report must reflect this.

The following description is written primarily with a delinquency case in mind and must be amended to conform to the special requirements of an abuse or neglect evaluation (see also Chapters 12 and 13).

A. History of Current Problem(s)

The current problem is analogous to the "chief complaint" of the standard medical and psychiatric history. Here it includes a history of both the legal problems and the psychiatric concerns. After noting the formal charge leading to the request for assessment, the report should state, making use of verbatim statements, how the juvenile perceives the problem. "They say I had something to do with the robbery" or "My lawyer sent me" are examples.

The youth's further elaboration of the current problems and his or her awareness of the charges and their implications are important. In particular, it should be noted whether the charges are admitted to or denied.

Recent medical, psychiatric, social, or educational problems and any obvious connection to the issues that have brought the adolescent to the court are noted. If a mental disorder is present, the onset and course of symptoms and signs should be given, along with details about recent treatments and their results. Similarly, any pattern of recent antisocial behavior should be detailed, along with its relationship to other areas of personality functioning.

The examiner must remain aware throughout the history taking that many details, especially those involving delinquent behavior, may be withheld, distorted, or denied. Therefore, the credibility of the youth's account is of major concern, as it often determines the reliability of the conclusions reached (see below). Here, mention should be made of this and a sense given of how well the juvenile's story held together.

B. Past Personal History

Aspects from the past history elicited in the evaluation are selected for the psychiatric report.

1. Family history. Family history should provide identifying data about siblings, half siblings, and different family configurations and living arrangements. Significant positive and negative relationships and periods of stress or disruptions in the integrity of the family are noted. A chronology of family moves and separations may be useful. Parental divorce, remarriages, arrivals and departures of family members, and significance of grandparents or stepparents are all important. What have been the strengths and weaknesses in the family should be noted. Socioeconomic status and religious background are essential data. Past clinical contacts or hospitalizations of family members are noted. Of major importance are the family's disciplinary practices, especially who had prime responsibility for administering punishment and what methods were used. Were these methods effective? Did they ever become cruel or sadistic? Could one describe the family as abusive? Was the youth before the court singled out for punishment? *Youth's dealing w these critical*

2. School history. School history should review both the scholastic performance and the behavior of the youth. An erratic history of doing well at one time and poorly at another may have special importance. Aggressive behavior and persistent truancy should be noted. Past psychological testing may provide valuable information. Attendance records, attitude about school, frequent shifts in schools, and special education classes may be relevant items.

3. Personal and social histories. Personal and social histories should include interrelationships within the family, if those are not covered in the family history section. Note the quality of relationships with peers of both sexes, whether any close friendships exist, and whether the youth tends to be a leader or follower. Activities outside of school (e.g., in the neighborhood, community centers, athletics, church affiliation) give a sense of how rich the life of the youth may be. Membership in a gang and whether it is a violent gang is vital information. The impact on the juvenile of particular peer role models and adverse influences from other youths or adults are included, e.g., "It was at the playground where we first started using drugs." The degree to which drug use is an organized group activity as opposed to a solo practice gives a sense of the neighborhood that the youth may have to return to.

4. Substance abuse history. In addition to the above, note the use of alcohol in terms of pattern, frequency, and so forth. Also note whether drug use has led to dependency or addiction and its connection to delinquent behavior (see Chapter 11).

5. Developmental and medical history. The developmental and medical history should review the standard developmental landmarks and stages (noting deviations from the norms), significant childhood illnesses, neurological disorders, chronic conditions such as juvenile diabetes, and so forth. Attention-deficit hyperactivity disorder is of particular importance, as is reference to medication prescribed for this or other dysfunctions. Special learning disabilities have been associated with delinquency and should be detailed. Psychosomatic illnesses may have occurred, and asthma and allergies may be highly significant. The reaction to an illness or accident might be directly or symbolically linked to antisocial behavior.

6. Psychiatric history. The psychiatric history should review previously diagnosed disorders and any treatment received, including all medications. Hospitalization and outpatient treatment and any information about their effectiveness should be outlined. Other early clinical syndromes may be especially relevant to the current behavior, including behavioral problems in infancy, eating or sleep disturbances, school refusal, enuresis, fire setting, cruelty to animals, or running away from home. Relevant aspects of the juvenile's sexual development and history can be included here. This area will receive particular attention in cases of sexual abuse or rape (see Chapter 13).

7. Legal history. The legal history includes past juvenile court appearances, adjudications, and dispositions; child custody disputes; or whether the juvenile was a victim of physical or sexual abuse. The youth may detail antisocial activity that never came to the attention of the court. Has the child ever had to be a witness in any proceeding? It may be desirable to include any type of antisocial or criminal record of immediate family members here as well.

C. Mental Status Examination

As noted in Chapter 6, the mental status examination used with juveniles differs from that used with adults. For one thing, the different ages of the minors being examined require a knowledge of developmental stages. What may be pathological in an adult can be within normal limits in an adolescent or child. There may be greater variability in how children and adolescents present, so differences observed on successive contacts should be pointed out. The standard mental status examination (see Appendix 7) must be adapted to the age of the patient and placed in a developmental context.

The general impression, speech pattern, mood and affect, ideational content, and manner of relating to others are important and are contained in this part of the examination. They provide a snap impression of the juvenile at one moment in time. Does the youth express any remorse, and does this remorse appear to be genuine? Manifest anger and/or hostility are exceedingly important, and any associated thoughts should be noted in detail, particularly in delinquency involving crimes against the person. Fantasies and dreams that may be pertinent to the charges are important to record. Sexual material might be included at this point.

D. Psychological Testing

If done, a summary of the results of tests administered should be provided, highlighting those features that *add* to the data garnered from the clinical interviews and that cast light on the questions raised by the court.

E. Interviews and Contacts With Family and Significant Others

In some jurisdictions, family interviews may not always be possible or allowed in juvenile delinquency cases. They can, however, be very useful as a complement to the information obtained from the youth and other sources. They provide another important perspective. The parents' perception of their child, their attitude toward the charges, and any evidence of psychopathology in members of the family may all be valuable contributions to an understanding of the youth. In child abuse and neglect situations, the parents must, of course, be examined, and a full psychiatric evaluation should be done and reported.

Occasionally, statements made by other relatives or friends of the juvenile may be important and should be incorporated in the report.

III. Diagnostic Formulation

The basis for a determination of the diagnosis is the American Psychiatric Association's *Diagnostic and Statistical Manual of Mental Disorders, Third Edition, Revised* (DSM-III-R). This is primarily a descriptive diagnostic nomenclature based on "objective" criteria such as signs, symptoms, and observable behavior rather than inferences. No particular personality theory is adopted. Diagnoses recorded in the report can include psychoses, developmental disorders, personality disorders, conduct disturbances, and various other conditions that may apply to the particular case. In a given case, the clinical picture may not fit neatly into any of the DSM-III-R categories. Examples are mixed or newly described syndromes. In such instances, a careful description of what is present is the best solution. Any physical diagnoses that are present should be added, and their relevance to the behavior that has gotten the juvenile into difficulties should be noted.

It is most important for the purposes of the court that the examiner develop the rationale for the diagnoses chosen. What may be self-evident to a mental health professional probably requires careful elaboration for the lawyers and judge. The thoughtful clinician knows that diagnosis is much more than a label and that typology alone cannot distinguish one patient from another in a meaningful way. For example, in many cases, a psychodynamic formulation will be appropriate and even necessary for answering the questions before the court or to assist the attorneys who are seeking an explanation for the youth's behavior. Two killings that, on the surface, seem to have been perpetrated in a cold, callous manner may have quite different clinical and legal significance. These differences will only be clarified by elucidating the underlying psychodynamic factors. One juvenile charged with homicide may appear indifferent, cynical, and aloof, whereas another may be guilt-ridden and depressed and may have been suicidal before the homicide. Needless to say, the meaning of the act may be entirely different for these two youths, and the appropriate disposition may be very different as well.

IV. Summary of Psychiatric Findings and Discussion of Legal Questions and Recommendations

From a legal standpoint, this section may be the most important part of the report. It is, unfortunately, often one of the weakest. The summary should be succinct and to the point, highlighting the major psychiatric findings that are pertinent to the formulation of dispositional recommendations. Clinical reasoning is then brought to bear on the diverse questions that the psychiatrist is being asked to address. The panoply of questions may touch on waiver, certification, dangerousness, treatability, credibility, and general personality assessment. It is exceedingly important in this section to distinguish facts from opinion. Reports written primarily in the form of conclusions, especially if not backed up by facts, are examples of psychiatry at its worst.

Each question raised by the court should be addressed independently, and pertinent clinical findings should be brought together to document the basis for every opinion expressed. The relevance of the diagnosis to the questions before the court should be spelled out and explained. Information garnered from third parties (as opposed to direct observation) is technically hearsay to a lawyer and even in juvenile court will not carry the same weight. One must be careful not to accept such information as fact. At best, it may amount to reasonable assumptions and should be so presented.

Though it may be difficult to apply psychiatric thinking to the realm of legal questions, that is precisely what is required. Some advocate a report that discusses conflicting opinions and allows the reader to reach his or her own conclusions. Usually, however, the examiner is expected to put forth his or her own personal analysis and be prepared to defend it as effectively as possible. Where important information is unavailable, one should explain how having it might change an opinion (for example, when an adolescent has a history of past psychiatric hospitalization and the records have not been made available). Making a case for diminished responsibility is hampered in such an instance.

> A 14-year-old boy in a correctional facility for larceny offenses is reported by his group therapist to have mentioned being sexually molested by a 17-year-old boy in his neighborhood before his institutionalization. On that basis, a complaint was brought via the group therapist to her supervisor, to a child protection worker, and to the county attorney's office. The 17-year-old was subsequently charged in the juvenile system for sexually molesting the younger boy. A psychiatrist was asked to assess the 17-year-old with regard to his propensity for sexually dangerous behavior and to propose a treatment plan. The 17-year-old denied the allegations and was unwilling to participate in a treatment program for sexual offenders. The psychiatrist is in a dilemma, particularly if the court tells the examining psychiatrist to assume that the facts are true. Even if the court has made a finding of sexual delinquency, the psychiatrist is placed in the awkward position of having to rely on information obtained in another setting while having no access to the complainant. This does not allow for a level of clinical certitude with which the clinician can be comfortable. Such limitations need to be made clear.

It may not be possible to answer every legal question asked, but it is necessary to explain why a question cannot be answered. One should also exercise caution about expanding the opinion section into areas not strictly germane to the issues before the court. Gratuitous comments about legal defenses that should be considered, sentencing alternatives, and idle speculations about events that may have occurred go beyond the expertise of a psychiatrist and must be avoided.

If specific recommendations are made, a strong, lucid statement can go a long way toward convincing the court to implement the recommendations made by the examiner. Obviously, input from a variety of other sources will figure in the final disposition.

Recommendations must be buttressed by well-reasoned arguments and may aim for the optimal placement but must ultimately be locally feasible (see Chapter 9). They should allow for temporary alternatives if the desired placement is not immediately available. The psychiatrist does not help the court by putting forth suggestions that cannot be implemented. When placement is the issue, it is often advisable to recommend a class rather than a specific facility, e.g., "a residential treatment center such as X."

Table 7–2 provides a checklist for use in formulating a psychiatric report.

Table 7–2.   Psychiatric report checklist

---

1. Have the sources of information and other documents relied on been listed?

2. Has all the relevant material from the history and psychiatric examination been included?

3. Has a summary of psychological testing been included when tests have been administered?

4. Has psychiatric jargon been avoided?

5. Have the answers to the legal questions been buttressed by the pertinent facts and carefully elucidated reasoning?

6. Are there questions that could not be answered? Which ones could not be answered, and why?

7. Have the psychiatric diagnoses been explained and made understandable to a judge and an attorney?

8. Does the summary highlight the important psychiatric findings and make clear their importance?

9. Have the following been clearly distinguished in the body of the report?

   • Factual material from inferences based on these facts
   • Opinions and hypotheses from facts or demonstrated conclusions based on steps of reasoning
   • The opinions of others when these have been relied on to form one's own conclusions

10. If recommendations have been made, has the rationale for them been made clear?

CHAPTER 8

COURT TESTIMONY: THE PSYCHIATRIST AS WITNESS

Richard A. Ratner, M.D.
Sandra G. Nye, J.D., M.S.W.

Although giving testimony is infrequently required in juvenile court cases, the psychiatrist who becomes involved in juvenile court must always be prepared to do so. The cases most likely to require testimony include those involving transfer, termination of parental rights, and custody issues.

A nonlawyer involved in a court proceeding often finds himself or herself frustrated by what appears to be a mysterious, quixotic, inefficient, and inhumane process. Clinicians find the "gamesmanship" and adversarial atmosphere particularly distressing. When called as witnesses, they frequently complain that they are attacked and made fools of and are not allowed to tell what they know. This is all the more intolerable when the court's decision is contrary to the clinician's view of what ought to be the outcome. Indeed, to a clinician, a court is an alien and hostile arena unless and until she or he understands the role of the legal system in our society, what a trial is, and what a trial is intended to accomplish.

The notion of testifying in juvenile court, even though the proceedings are in general far less adversarial than those in the adult system, is therefore distasteful and even frightening to many mental health professionals who are not familiar with the experience. Many will avoid taking cases that are before the court because of the concern that testimony may be required later on. This is unfortunate because of the need of the court system for competent evaluations on which it can base wise and humane dispositions.

The range of the intensity, sophistication, and vigor of the testimony varies widely from jurisdiction to jurisdiction and case to case. Testifying in juvenile court need not be a traumatic experience when the psychiatrist has done a careful and competent assessment and report so that the groundwork for persuasive, useful testimony has already been laid. This chapter will attempt to describe and clarify the experience of testifying in order to demystify the process and to assist the practitioner in maximizing his or her effectiveness in court.

THE PRACTITIONER AS EXPERT WITNESS

Two categories of witness may come before the court: the fact, lay, or occurrence witness and the expert witness. The lay witness is called to testify because of information that is in his or her possession with regard to a particular case. He or she is allowed to testify only to the facts as she or he knows them and is not permitted to offer opinions. By contrast, an expert witness is used to help the court analyze, interpret, and make decisions about the facts that have been established; hence his or her expert opinions are not only permitted but sought by the court.

Fact witnesses to a crime may include victims, police officers, or bystanders who have overheard incriminating information. Mental health professionals may also be called as fact, rather than expert, witnesses. Typically, mental health professionals who are called as fact witnesses are usually current or past treating psychiatrists and have information about the juvenile, such as his or her mental state, that is germane to the matter at hand. Thus, even though one is expert in the field of psychiatry, one may be called as a lay witness.

For a psychiatrist, the distinction between what is "information" and what is expertise may be obscure at best, but there are important distinctions between serving as a lay witness versus an expert witness. Lay witnesses have no choice in the matter of whether to appear in court; if summoned, they must appear. They are paid a nominal sum for their appearance, perhaps $25 per day. Unless they are also accepted as "experts" by the court, they must avoid giving opinions.

In contrast, a psychiatrist who appears as an expert has agreed to perform an evaluation fully aware of the possibility that testimony may be required. The court appearance is either part of his or her regular duties as an employee of the court clinic, or if he or she is a private practitioner, the court appearance is paid for at an hourly rate closer to ordinary psychiatric fees. The rationale for this special treatment is that the expert witness is special. By virtue of education, training, skill, and experience, he or she can guide the court in its attempts to make just decisions (1).

INDEPENDENT COURT'S WITNESS OR ADVERSARY EXPERT

An expert may be called either as an independent "court's witness" (a neutral professional chosen by the court or by agreement of the parties) or an adversary expert for one or the other side in the case. Independent witnesses are typically practitioners who are salaried employees of the court or who staff clinics that contract with the court to perform evaluations. Although an independent witness owes no allegiance to either party to the proceedings, she or he may be subject to cross-examination by *both* sides, depending on the expert's conclusions.

An adversary witness, by contrast, is hired by one side in the dispute in the hope that his or her findings will be helpful to that side of the case. Because it is not possible to know before an evaluation whether one will feel able to testify on behalf of the side that initiated the contact, it is recommended that the psychiatrist have a clear understanding with the attorney at the outset: the psychiatrist agrees only to evaluate the case and decide whether or not to serve as an expert witness; the clinician will be paid for the time in evaluating the case and consulting with the attorney whether or not he or she agrees to testify. It is common practice, and in no way unethical, to require payment in advance (a retainer) to cover the evaluation.

THE ADVERSARIAL PROCESS AND THE JUVENILE COURT

For much of its history the juvenile court system functioned more as a social welfare agency dedicated to the rehabilitation of juveniles than as a criminal court. It did not borrow much from the adversarial system found in adult criminal courts. To the degree that this is still the case, i.e., where the *parens patriae* (state as parent) position prevails, testimony is apt to be more informal, even friendly. Each lawyer attempts to have the psychiatrist provide a consultation-like presentation to the court to further the court's in-depth understanding of the youth. In other courts, a more formal examination and cross-examination occur in all cases.

Juvenile court philosophy and practice have changed significantly in the past 30 years through such seminal Supreme Court decisions as *In re Gault* and *Kent v. United States* (see Appendix 5). The direction of change has been toward the provision of greater due process safeguards to juvenile defendants. These due process safeguards are achieved by greater reliance on the adversarial process. As a result, the juvenile court increasingly has come to resemble the adult criminal court.

From the standpoint of the witness, testimony in an adversarial setting is far more rigorous and stressful than in the more traditional juvenile court setting. The side calling the witness will pursue a "friendly" direct examination aimed at bolstering the witness's credentials and permitting the witness to describe in detail his or her assessment and resulting opinions. The opposing side, however, will seek to attack not only the conclusions and recommendations reached by the witness but the credentials and methods as well.

PREPARATION FOR HEARING

Usually a witness is made aware informally that testimony will be needed in court, but formal notification of the actual date and time is often by subpoena. This document may appear formidable, but it should not be intimidating. It may or may not be issued by the attorney for the party whom the witness favors or who has hired him or her. The witness should contact the "friendly side's" lawyer to arrange, if possible, a mutually convenient time for appearing in court and to arrange for a preparation conference. The conference has two purposes: it permits the psychiatrist to educate the attorney about relevant mental health concepts in general and his or her views regarding the current case in particular, and it allows the attorney to prepare the psychiatrist for both the direct examination and the expected cross-examination by the opposing attorney.

Attorneys working in juvenile court are often overburdened and may be ill prepared to present a case. The psychiatrist may need to be forceful in demanding time to review the content and strategy of testimony with counsel. It is most important to understand the legal concepts underlying the case so that the testimony will be relevant to the specific issues being tried. For example, in a custody hearing, the best interests of the child may be the standard for the court's decision, and it is about these best interests that the court will wish to hear. In a termination of parental rights hearing, however, the fitness of the parent may be the only issue, and the child's interests may not be at issue. The psychiatrist can be very helpful to the attorney by providing textbook or journal articles and verbally explaining the psychiatric issues. At the same time, the attorney should be asked to provide the psychiatrist with law journal or similar articles, or even published court opinions on the relevant law.

THE "QUALIFYING" OF THE EXPERT

Before a witness is allowed to testify as to opinions, it must be demonstrated to the court that she or he meets the requirements for an expert witness. The standards for expertise vary from one community to another, based largely on the availability of clinical witnesses. Neighboring counties may have different criteria for expert witness qualification. Also, it is entirely possible that a well-credentialed professional who is recognized as an expert in his or her field may not be accepted by the court as an expert in a given case.

A father's treating psychiatrist was called as a witness in a child sexual abuse case. On cross-examination by the prosecutor, the doctor testified that he was not a child psychiatrist, had received no special training in child abuse, had never treated a case of child abuse, had no special training in sexual deviancy (including pedophilia and incest), and had never treated a sexual deviant. The court allowed him to testify as to some facts but refused to allow him to testify to his opinion as to whether or not the child had been sexually abused, what the effect on the child would be if she were permitted to live in her parents' home with her father, whether the father was a pedophile, or whether he was at risk for molesting the child or other children in the household again.

The process by which the court makes the determination as to whether or not to accept the witness as an expert is called "qualifying the expert." It involves the witness testifying under oath as to credentials, education, postgraduate training, professional clinical and faculty affiliations, professional organization memberships and offices, recognitions and awards, publications, professional experience, and any other information that will convince the court not only that the person has professional expertise sufficient to enable the court to hear his or her opinion testimony, but also that the opinion should be given weight. The expert's resume will also be placed in evidence, and the opposing counsel will have been given an opportunity to view and to corroborate it. Therefore, the resume should be up to date, absolutely accurate, and detailed. It is not always necessary that a psychiatrist has had specialized training or experience to be qualified by the court as an expert. A common question is, "How many cases of this nature have you seen or treated?" If the answer is "none" or "only a few," the attorney should be forewarned. He or she will then skip that question, or couch it in such terms that the lack of direct experience is unimportant, and will inquire instead as to the witness's familiarity with the clinical concepts and literature relating to the condition that is at issue. This is usually sufficient to qualify the doctor as an expert. If, on the other hand, the opposing expert has specialized knowledge and vast experience in this very area, his or her testimony will doubtless be given much greater weight. A party's hiring of an expert vastly credentialed, experienced, and renowned is an indicator for an equal expert on the other side. There is no shame in being younger or having experience confined to some other clinical area, but one may not wish to compete against a much more senior colleague. Every potential expert witness should consider this possibility, if there is the opportunity, before agreeing to enter the fray.

DIRECT EXAMINATION

Once the witness is accepted as an expert in the case, direct examination proceeds, conducted by the attorney who has called the witness. The purpose of direct testimony is to put the facts before the judge in a thorough and convincing manner. Through a series of questions, the expert will be asked about his or her entry into the case, the nature of the evaluation, the conclusions reached, and in most courts, his or her opinions as to the outcome of the case. The formal, approved style for the question is, "Have you an opinion, doctor, based on a reasonable degree of psychiatric certainty as to ___?" The correct answer is "yes" or "no." If "yes," the next question is, "What is your opinion?" After the response, the lawyer will inquire, "What is the basis of your opinion?" The expert now has the opportunity to inform the court as to the clinical issues and should fully describe all major aspects of his or her report. Lawyers employ widely varied styles of examination, but research indicates that a witness's conclusions are most effective if presented early in the testimony, followed by explanation and elaboration, or toward the end after a foundation has been laid. The conclusions should not be buried somewhere in the middle, where they can be easily overlooked.

Occasionally, an expert will be asked to testify as to an opinion based not on his or her own examination of a person but on a hypothetical question. The question will contain all facts and details already testified to on the issue about which the opinion is sought. The form of the question is, "Doctor, I ask you to assume (e.g., a male child, aged 6 years, who, etc.). . . . Doctor, assuming these facts, have you an opinion, based on a reasonable degree of psychiatric certainty, as to ___?"

In some jurisdictions, case law or the hearing officer's preference may preclude expert testimony as to the "ultimate issues" before the court, e.g., whether the individual is or is not competent or criminally responsible. The prepared witness will have ascertained whether such testimony is permitted or desired.

CROSS-EXAMINATION

Cross-examination is the bugaboo of every witness. Its purpose is to probe the witness's knowledge, expertise, findings, and conclusions with the intent of discrediting or minimizing them. This process is called "impeachment." In this context, impeachment means an effort to destroy, if possible, or at least diminish the witness's credibility and the weight and effectiveness of the testimony. It may feel to the witness that the cross-examiner is given far too much latitude in this regard, but these tactics are quite legal unless they become abusive. Experience will inure the expert witness to this process. Although the witness feels intimidated and badgered under cross-examination, it is important to keep in mind that the opposing attorney is simply doing a job and does not intend a personal attack. All of the psychiatrist authors of this handbook have had the experience of being the subject of a blistering cross-examination by an attorney who later contacted him or her about acting as an expert in another of the attorney's cases. If an expert has done a careful and thoughtful job and offers opinions candidly and modestly, the cross-examiner may accomplish little in the attack. It is important in this regard that the witness remain professional and dignified in bearing, regardless of the intensity of the questioning.

No attorney is as well versed in the area of mental health as is a psychiatrist. Most attorneys will recognize that and avoid getting too deeply into discussions of psychiatric concepts. On the other hand, sometimes an opposing attorney has been coached by another mental health professional and may accordingly show surprising sophistication in his or her line of questioning. Regardless of what is actually brought up in cross-examination, the expert will be rewarded by responding in a patient and unruffled manner. Skillful handling of cross-examination is especially challenging and can be a rewarding professional experience. Once oriented to the courtroom, the mental health professional may come to feel satisfied with his or her performance more often than not and even enjoy the intellectual joust.

REDIRECT AND RECROSS EXAMINATION

Redirect examination permits the attorney who calls a witness to clarify issues or to "repair" any damage done by the cross-examination. Recross is usually brief and must be limited to issues raised in redirect examination. At the termination of the attorneys' examinations, the judge may ask questions. When the judge has finished doing so, the testimony has ended and the witness is directed to step down. A witness may not leave the courtroom until "excused" by the judge. Once that happens, the witness should leave promptly. To remain in the courtroom as a spectator gives the appearance of either overinvolvement in the matter or having nothing important to do.

KEYS TO WITNESS EFFECTIVENESS

The weight given an expert's opinion depends substantially on the overall impression that the expert makes. Such factors as eminence in one's field, a large number of publications, or skill with patients may be far less important than one's persuasiveness in the courtroom.

To be believable, one should look the part. Attire should be conservative, and one should be well groomed. Tardiness to court is irritating and will start the expert off on the wrong foot. On the stand, one should maintain a relaxed and confident posture and avoid fidgeting and gesturing, to the extent possible. Responses should be directed to the judge or, if there should happen to be one, the jury.

An invaluable learning source for a witness is a stack of transcripts of other expert testimony. Training videotapes are also available (2). An important part of witness preparation is understanding the legal concepts in the case so that the testimony can be directed accordingly. The expert should keep in mind that she or he is speaking to laypersons and should phrase the presentation accordingly. It is advisable to steer clear of jargon and explain terms when presenting one's findings in a clear and cogent fashion.

Whether the witness is testifying on direct or cross-examination, there are some time-honored techniques for effective testimony:

- Just answer the question; never volunteer anything. Prearrange a signal with the attorney for whose side you are testifying to alert him or her if the question as asked requires that more be said and you want him or her to ask another question by way of eliciting more detail or clarifying the testimony.
- Never answer an ambiguous question or a question containing misinformation. Rather than assuming the examiner's intent, ask for clarification or repetition of the question before responding.
- Pause a moment before answering each question. This has the effect of capturing the judge's attention and gives you time to reflect. On cross-examination, it breaks the rhythm of the cross-examiner's questions, particularly if she or he uses a rapid-fire technique as a method of disconcerting you; it also gives the friendly attorney an opportunity to interpose an objection to an improper question, which could be very important.
- Avoid defensiveness in responding.
- Never guess at an answer, refuse to admit the obvious, or descend into argument with the examiner.
- Be cautious in claiming or acknowledging any text, article, or textbook as the authority for your theory or conclusion. To do so is a trap that may later require having to try to explain a disagreement or inconsistency with a quote, possibly taken out of context, from the source you claim as authoritative. One may acknowledge a work as well known or considered by some to be authoritative and still disagree with all or some portion of it, explaining that there are other theories on the point, or differentiating this case from the quoted position. If you think the author is just plain wrong, you may simply say that you disagree. The expert should make it clear that his or her knowledge is broadly based on training and experience as well as the literature.
- If you are being badgered, use your prearranged signal to alert your attorney to intervene. In a pinch, turn to the judge for direction or protection.

RULES OF EVIDENCE

In some juvenile courts, the rules of evidence are relaxed. In courts where they are strictly enforced, rules of evidence apply to every litigant equally and create a matrix within which the trial must be conducted. They are intended to ensure fairness and honesty by accepting as evidence only facts (not speculations or beliefs) that are material (information that has bearing on the matter in dispute) and relevant (information that tends to prove a material fact) and that a witness, sworn to tell the truth, knows of his or her own knowledge to be true (not hearsay).

The constraint placed on testimony by the rules of evidence causes considerable frustration for witnesses who have a story to tell and want to be allowed simply to tell it. The law gathers information very differently from the clinical sciences because it is interested only in objective facts and not subjective reality.

Hearsay and Its Exceptions

A witness is allowed to testify only to facts that he or she knows. Unless an exception to the hearsay rule applies, he or she may not testify to the truth of facts gleaned from other sources, e.g., statements, records, or other information made or prepared by persons other than the witness. Statements made outside the courtroom and not under oath are hearsay. This limitation may put a clinician at a considerable disadvantage in testifying because much of what a clinician relies on to arrive at a conclusion as to the facts in a case would be designated hearsay by a court. A witness may testify to the fact that a person made a particular statement (testifying to the verbal act), but not to the truth of that statement.

> In a child abuse case in which the victim is preverbal, the mother and other children in the family tell the clinician that the father beat the child. This is verified by the cringing reaction of the child when confronted with the father (certainly not always the case). The clinician may not testify to the fact that the father beat the child; the clinician may testify to his or her opinion that the child has been traumatized, if that is the case and an opinion is asked for. If asked the basis for the opinion, she or he may testify to all of the facts and information that have led to the conclusion, including the statements of the mother and children. If, for example, the mother and other children are for some reason not available to testify to the beating they witnessed, or if they have recanted (perhaps out of fear of the father or fear of being without him), the fact that they have made the statements (verbal acts) in the past may be testified to.

Clinical records and hearsay problems. In some jurisdictions, clinical records are admissible in evidence under a business records exception to the rule against hearsay. The business records exception is based on the theory that records kept in the ordinary course of business may be presumed accurate. Other jurisdictions may recognize the business records exception but exclude clinical records from it. How, then, can relevant, necessary information contained in clinical records be placed before the court? Admissibility of clinical records will vary from one jurisdiction to another and the facts in a given situation.

Some states have adopted a form of Rule 7 of the Federal Rules of Evidence (3), which permits an expert to testify as to the basis of his or her opinion. Information that would otherwise be excluded as hearsay may be testified to by the expert if it was relied on by him or her in arriving at an opinion and is the type of information generally relied on by those in the field. For example, facts recounted by a mother or teacher in the course of an evaluation of a child could be testified to by the expert under this rule, although the expert would not otherwise be allowed to testify to those facts because they are hearsay. If the jurisdiction does not recognize such an exception, the mother or teacher would have to be called as a witness to produce those facts, which might be cumbersome or impossible in a particular case. It is to be remembered that testimony as to facts recounted by others will not be allowed unless the expert first testifies that he or she relied on that information in arriving at his or her opinion and it is the type of information generally relied on by experts in the field in arriving at their opinions.

Another exception to the hearsay rule is what is known as *res gestae*. Statements made shortly after an occurrence, particularly if they are of a dramatic or startling nature, are assumed to be true. For this reason, they may be testified to as an exception to the hearsay rule. Similarly, statements made by a patient in the course of receiving treatment (distinguished from information given for forensic purposes) are assumed to be true and may be allowed. (For example, the treating clinician may be allowed to testify to the facts of an instance of abuse recounted by the child shortly after the occurrence.)

If a witness cannot recall details that have been recorded, such as dates or precisely who said what, notes that were made contemporaneously with the event or shortly thereafter might be admissible in evidence as past recollections recorded. This situation would come up when the witness is asked a question and responds that he or she does not remember. The questioner will inquire whether his or her recollection is exhausted. If the answer is affirmative, the witness will be asked whether there is anything that could refresh his or her recollection. If a review of the notes is sufficient, the witness will be allowed to look at them and then testify from memory. If that is not sufficient, and the witness can state that the notes meet the requirements of contemporaneity and accuracy, the record itself may be admitted into evidence. This is often very helpful, but there is one caveat: the other side will have an opportunity to review the material and cross-examine the witness on the basis of it.

Before a witness will be allowed to testify as to a conversation, and before a document will be permitted into evidence, the witness must lay a foundation for admission. In the case of a conversation, the witness will be asked when and where the conversation took place, who was there, and what was said. Similarly, to authenticate a document, the preparer of the document, or in some instances an official keeper of records, must testify to its authenticity and that it has not been altered.

SPECIAL ISSUES

Several issues may be encountered more frequently in juvenile court than in other court settings. For example, because much of the legal representation in juvenile court is done by public lawyers who are shockingly overworked, a witness may not be able to meet with the attorney responsible for the direct examination, despite the best of intentions. As a result, the attorney may conduct a rambling, confused, or illogical direct examination that will be frustrating to all participants. Although the request may not necessarily be granted, the witness in such a circumstance should be assertive in asking permission to organize the testimony in the preferred order.

One of the most difficult tasks for an expert is testifying about a parent's deficits or psychopathology in the parent's presence. Schetky and Benedek (4) have recommended several approaches to this dilemma. For example, they suggest looking at the parent while describing a strength, while directing other testimony to the judge. The burden may also be decreased by depicting the parents as victims of abuse, poor parenting, or serious deprivation, conveying empathy for their circumstances while describing their capabilities and vulnerabilities. The small size of many juvenile courtrooms, and the closeness of the parties' and counsel's tables, may intensify this problem. While waiting to testify, the witness can at least choose to sit in a secluded area (perhaps outside the courtroom) to avoid direct confrontation with the parent(s).

The complexity of testimony may be increased by the number of attorneys questioning the witness. Each party has counsel and possibly a guardian ad litem (see Chapter 4, p. 22). A guardian ad litem may also be present for the children. In some jurisdictions, foster parents may also be present with counsel. The witness should make sure that the attorneys identify themselves and their roles, so the witness may better focus on the relevant issues as questions are posed.

The structure of juvenile court, including the exigencies of the court's schedule and budget, may limit the scope of the evaluation. The evaluator should perform an evaluation at least sufficient to form an opinion for testimony but may need to acknowledge frankly certain data limitations.

In addition to the limitations of the data, the witness should be ready to answer questions about the availability or limitations of mental health services to treat certain disorders such as severe personality or conduct disorders. Questions will also be raised about the clinician's ability to predict (i.e., the prognosis of an illness or behavior). The witness should be informed about the limitations of long-term prediction and about relevant literature associating patterns of juvenile behaviors with adult antisocial activities. Emphasis should be placed on past behavior being the best predictor of future behavior, particularly if the parent or youth has not used services to make any changes.

Witnesses must understand the limitations of the use of mental health testimony to establish the credibility of an allegation. For example, testimony on offender profiles or other classifications of abusers has always been deemed by appellate courts to be inadmissible as prejudicial. A mental health professional called to testify as to the characteristics of abusive parents is ethically required to describe the limitations of the literature and the overlap among populations. The witness should also state the difficulties in drawing inferences about individual events on the basis of group data. Similarly, there has been disapproval of opinion evidence about the credibility of children in general. A few states permit testimony regarding the credibility of individual abuse victims. More widely accepted is testimony explaining child development concepts, behaviors of abused children, or dynamics of the abusive situation. Witnesses should clarify those issues on which they are to testify, as well as whether their testimony can be helpful and whether they can participate ethically.

REFERENCES

1. Bank SC, Poythress NG Jr: The elements of persuasion in expert testimony. Journal of Psychiatry and the Law 10(2):173–204, 1982
2. American Academy of Psychiatry and the Law, Learning Resources Center, 1211 Cathedral Street, Baltimore, MD 21201. 1-800-331-1389.
3. Federal Rules of Evidence 7
4. Schetky DH, Benedek EP (eds): Child Psychiatry and the Law. New York, Brunner/Mazel, 1980

CHAPTER 9

DISPOSITION

Michael G. Kalogerakis, M.D.

The third stage of a juvenile court proceeding, after intake and adjudication, is disposition. All prior activity in the court is but a prelude to this endpoint, when the court decides what is to be done. It is the most important consequence of an appearance in court. It is disposition that concerns the juvenile most, particularly with regard to whether the youth will be "sent away." The family, too, wants to know what the outcome of all the legal deliberations will be. Is the child to be returned to their care? If so, under what conditions? Will the child or the parents be expected to participate in some treatment program? Of what kind?

For some authors, disposition is also the most critical phase for the mental health professional. For example, Fitch, though a lawyer, stated, "Without a doubt, the most significant contribution that the mental health community can make to the juvenile justice process is to identify the needs of troubled youths and to provide services responsive to those needs" (1, p. 160).

Lawyers for the child ultimately focus most of their energies on the disposition phase. The defense lawyer has a particular concern for the child's right to be at liberty, i.e., to be returned to the care of the family and not to be placed against his or her will. Many lawyers are equally eager to ensure that their client will obtain needed services. It must be noted that some attorneys, as a matter of philosophy, are opposed to any interference with the autonomy of their client, regardless of what may seem to be the client's clinical needs. As a consequence, they will seldom request a psychiatric evaluation.

The range of dispositions possible partly depends on the resources available in the particular community. The broader the range of services available, the easier it is to develop a helpful set of recommendations. Because the ideal is seldom found, many dispositions represent compromises.

Disposition of a case is a judicial decision, arrived at by pooling the information about the child and family from various sources, especially probation, social services, mental health, school records, law enforcement, and victims' statements. In addition, the prosecutor and the defense counsel may submit requests for specific dispositions. The contributions of the mental health professional may be of vital importance, notably in cases where the child or parents are emotionally disturbed. For the psychiatrist, the formulation of recommendations is the natural product of a diagnostic evaluation, i.e., the treatment plan toward which all training is directed.

The core of a psychiatric evaluation is the diagnostic formulation described in Chapter 6. One part of that formulation is the diagnosis itself, which is a descriptive label from the American Psychiatric Association's *Diagnostic and Statistical Manual of Mental Disorders, Third Edition, Revised* (DSM-III-R). It is important to point out that diagnosis per se is insufficient information on which to base an adequate treatment plan. For example, one schizophrenic may require hospitalization for an extended period, whereas another may be easily managed in the community with the appropriate support services. Similarly, one adolescent diagnosed as having a conduct disorder may require a highly controlled setting to function normally, whereas another with the same diagnosis but better impulse control may be able to function adequately with a looser structure and do quite well in a more open placement.

Aside from the issue of proper placement (where the guiding principle is the least restrictive setting that will still meet the needs of the child), numerous other determinations need to be made. Is the home a reasonably healthy setting to which the child may be safely returned? Is a normal school setting appropriate, or is special education needed? Does the assessment of strengths and weaknesses in a juvenile point to a need for special services such as psychiatric treatment? What kind of special services? What special problems does the youth present, e.g., the potential for serious aggression? Is he or she likely to be a threat to the community at large or only to specific individuals such as family members? Is such a potential for violence amenable to therapeutic intervention or not? What are the implications for further care of the youngster with limited intellectual development? What can we offer the inveterate recidivist?

In an abuse and neglect case, the primary issue in recommending a disposition is to maintain the child's safety. Secondarily, the assessment should lead to a diagnosis and interventions to aid in treating and maintaining the family, if at all possible. In recommending dispositions in such cases, the psychiatrist should assess the treatability of the parent(s) and the family system. The good, as well as the poor, prognostic signs for continued maltreatment of the child in the family should be cited. The mental health evaluation should identify any treatable causes of parenting problems (e.g., depression, substance abuse) and assess the parents' insight, motivation for treatment, and response to past interventions. Assessment should also elucidate the special needs of the child and whether these needs have made the child vulnerable to abuse.

The opinion section of reports on abuse and neglect cases should describe the parents' and child's psychopathology, the effect of the psychopathology on parenting, specific indicated social and mental health interventions, and methods of monitoring the progress of the family. In some cases it may be necessary to indicate that in the opinion of the examiner, the family is not treatable and permanent removal of the child is indicated. Because termination of parental rights is probably the most anguished decision a juvenile court judge ever has to make, most careful documentation of this recommendation is essential. (See Chapter 16.)

Knowledge of the various kinds of treatment settings and opportunities available locally is essential to a mental health professional working with youths before the court. The variety of treatment centers and their criteria for admission will vary greatly from one locality to another. The current status of a program with respect to openings is information that should be made available to the court because it must realistically figure in the recommendations being formulated. The psychiatrist may then be in communication with the placement office serving the court. In some jurisdictions, this may be the office of probation; in others, it may be the local social services agency.

The range of dispositions that may be used by the court include the following:

1. *Hospitalization,* which may short term or longer term. Short-term hospitalization is usually for 2 to 6 weeks, for the purpose of a psychiatric evaluation that cannot be properly performed in an outpatient setting. This placement is for youths who are too disturbed or too dangerous to be allowed to remain in the community. Longer-term hospitalization is usually for treatment that an evaluation has determined cannot be appropriately provided in a nonhospital setting (e.g., treatment for a psychotic or seriously suicidal youngster). A variant is an institution for the mentally retarded, when appropriate.
2. *Correctional institution* or training school. This placement is for juveniles who manifest no significant emotional disturbance, fall diagnostically in the category of conduct disorder, and present too great a risk to the community to be left in a less controlled setting. These youngsters generally lack the self-control not to run away from a less secure institution, have shown a persistent pattern of serious delinquency, may be violent, and have not been responsive to earlier treatment efforts.
3. *Residential treatment center.* This placement is for those who need treatment in a residential setting and can function with only a modicum of supervision and control. Youngsters who do not manifest serious psy-

chopathology but come from a disturbed home that is inimical to their optimum growth and development are sent here. Also, abused and neglected children often meet the criteria for this placement.

4. *Group home or community residence.* This placement is for those youngsters who would be able ordinarily to remain at home and attend school in the community but whose home is at least temporarily unable to meet their needs. The group home or community residence may include treatment opportunities such as group therapy or individual psychotherapy.

5. *Return home on probation, possibly with clinic follow-up.* By far the most common disposition, this may incorporate special education recommendations or specific therapeutic interventions (e.g., pharmacotherapy, behavior modification, family therapy). Other possibilities, depending on the nature of the problem, would include a drug rehabilitation center (or community-based program), a sex offender treatment program, medical treatment when a specific physical problem exists, and others.

6. In a few states, restitution (e.g., Maryland) and community service (e.g., California) may be imposed by the court.

7. Referral of the child to the Committee on Special Education in a public school system, under PL 94-142, the Education of All Handicapped Children Act.

Knowledge of the local laws governing hospitalization, institutions for the retarded, training schools, and other placements is also essential for drawing up proper dispositional recommendations for a disturbed youth. But if the law requires that the youth be mentally ill *and* dangerous to himself or herself or to others, such placement may be precluded and alternatives must be sought. These are often fine determinations requiring considerable expertise that only a properly trained and well-informed mental health professional can provide for mentally ill and dangerous youths.

When specific psychiatric treatment is indicated, the expert should spell out the modalities most likely to be useful. Is behavior modification the treatment of choice? This might be the case for many personality disorders where internal conflict with consequent anxiety is not a major finding. On the other hand, the youngster who manifests significant anxiety or is depressed could probably benefit from psychotherapy. If the youth's problems appear to be secondary to strife in the family, family therapy may be the treatment of choice. Agitation, which in some cases may spur a youth to commit crimes, might be adequately controlled with medication. The same is true when psychosis is present.

When recommending specific interventions, it is incumbent on the clinician to discuss the issue of treatability. Whether or not the clinician claims that the youth is treatable, a carefully drawn rationale with appropriate references to the literature will often help to convince the court to accept the recommendations.

A particularly thorny problem for the court is the juvenile with multiple diagnoses: for example, a mentally disturbed youth who shows symptoms of mental retardation or may be abusing drugs. What part of the system of care has prime responsibility? Is such responsibility readily acknowledged by the pertinent agency, or is the court likely to be caught in the middle of an interagency struggle? These are issues that must be primarily addressed and resolved by the responsible state and local agencies: first by the establishment of clear policies and guidelines and second by facilitating placement in the individual case, a process in which the court clinician may be of assistance.

Another chronic source of frustration to the court in virtually all parts of the country is the paucity of treatment resources that are available locally. One might well ask, what good does it do to draw up carefully designed dispositional recommendations if there is no way of implementing them? It is the responsibility of the psychiatrist evaluating a patient to formulate an ideal treatment plan, consistent with the present state of our knowledge. The recommendations might subsequently have to be adjusted to the local realities, but there will at least be a record of what the individual youth *should* have. Ultimately, government must decide whether to commit the funds to develop the services needed.

Although many youths who come before the court may not require a psychiatric evaluation or input from a psychiatrist at the point of disposition, in a number of instances the participation of the psychiatrist in the deliberations should be mandatory. All abuse and neglect cases should be evaluated. Other cases include, but are not limited to, psychotic youths, seriously suicidal or violent youths, repeat offenders (especially when there is a pattern of worsening delinquency), and sex offenders, where danger to the community may be an issue. In such cases, the court is especially interested in the youth's prognosis. Much has been written about psychiatrists' and psychologists' inability to predict dangerousness, and the American Psychiatric Association has taken a position that supports this perception (2). At the same time, all treatment plans are based in part on the prognosis, i.e., prediction of the likely course of the illness.

The court must make judgments based on its belief that the undesirable behavior will or will not continue under given circumstances. When the individual before the court has psychiatric problems, it is appropriate for the court to expect some statement regarding prognosis from the psychiatrist or other mental health professional. In no case will the expert's opinion represent a totally reliable prediction. Nonetheless, varying degrees of confidence are possible and can certainly be thoughtfully expressed to the court. This opinion, accompanied by appropriate caveats, can be an invaluable contribution to the judge, who has to make difficult decisions for which she or he lacks the expertise.

Other considerations that must be weighed by the court and kept in mind by the psychiatrist include the nature of the environment to which a youth would be returning if released. A high-crime neighborhood offers little opportunity for a well-motivated youngster to straighten out. For the drug abuser, freedom too often guarantees return to such abuse and a resulting downhill course. A chaotic or destructive home places an intolerable burden on a child already beleaguered by internal stress.

In formulating recommendations, a psychiatrist must give serious consideration to the rights of the juvenile, including the right to remain free in the community, to live at home with his or her family, and to obtain an education in a normal school setting. The psychiatrist can be as effective an advocate for the youth's civil rights as any of the other court personnel. Differences usually arise around the question of the youth's wishes, especially when these conflict with what the psychiatrist believes to be in the youth's best interests. This conflict is nowhere more evident than in cases of abuse where the child may express a fervent desire to return home.

What should be the position of the defense attorney? In delinquency matters, youths at odds with society and in conflict with their parents will frequently have different notions about what is best for them. It is the defense counsel's responsibility to represent the youth's desires before the court to the best of his or her ability. It is the psychiatrist's responsibility to determine whether those desires are the product of a mind mature and sound enough to conceptualize self-interest and to comprehend the rationale of a realistic treatment plan. The court is not serving the youth well if it places him or her in a setting that demands so much self-control that failure is foreordained. Thus youngsters who demonstrably lack the internal controls to resist the temptations of a high-crime neighborhood must be placed away from that neighborhood if they are to have a chance of straightening out their lives. By the same token, a youngster whose controls are poor and impulses dangerous (e.g., an arsonist) could pose a threat to other youths in an open residential treatment center. The youth will require a more secure setting with more intensive treatment. The psychiatrist must spell out clearly such reasoning and present the evidence on which it is based. This responsibility is identical to the one faced by the psychiatrist working in a hospital when discharge of a patient is being considered. Discharge planning necessarily involves prognostication. One assumes that the patient has improved sufficiently to manage his or her life in the community, but there is always a risk factor (3). Hopefully the risk can be reduced to the minimum by careful diagnosis and analysis of all relevant data.

From the mental health professional's standpoint, all treatment settings and modalities have something to offer, although any given facility may not be up to standard. The task facing the court is to choose the setting in which specific interventions can best be provided based on the given needs and disability of the youngster. The perfect match-up is a rarely achieved goal, partly because of limited resources and partly because of the limitations of our science. In all instances, a coordinated approach that pools the information and expertise of the various disciplines involved with the court-related youth offers the best hope of making the youth's appearance in court a worthwhile experience that can begin to turn his or her life around.

REFERENCES

1. Fitch WL: Competency to stand trial and criminal responsibility in the juvenile court, in Juvenile Homicide. Edited by Benedek EP, Cornell DG. Washington, DC, American Psychiatric Press, 1989, p 143–162
2. American Psychiatric Association: Clinical Aspects of the Violent Individual (Task Force Report No 8). Washington, DC, American Psychiatric Press, 1974, pp 23–30
3. Mathew v Nelson, 461 FSupp 707, 1978

WAIVER OR TRANSFER TO ADULT COURT

Kathleen M. Quinn, M.D.

Psychiatrists working in private practice, clinics, or juvenile court settings may be called on to examine a juvenile involved in a delinquency proceeding and to offer opinions about the suitability of treating the youth in programs offered within the juvenile justice system. This examination allows the mental health professional to have a major influence over whether a juvenile remains in juvenile court or is transferred to adult criminal court. Although most states give juvenile court exclusive jurisdiction over children charged with criminal acts, the power to transfer jurisdiction to adult court has always been a part of the juvenile justice system. This process of transferring jurisdiction has different names, including transfer hearing, waiver hearing, jurisdictional hearing, fitness hearing, or certification hearing. Whatever the label, the issues remain the same. To waive jurisdiction in most states, the court must find that the child or adolescent presents a danger to the public and/or that he or she is not amenable to treatment in programs offered within the juvenile justice system. If the case is transferred to adult criminal court, the juvenile complaint is dismissed.

On entry into the adult system, the juvenile is exposed to the same range of sanctions as an adult. There may be some restrictions, such as prohibition of the death penalty for minors, but the general effect of transfer is to treat the minor as if he or she were an adult. These proceedings are often viewed as a recognition that the juvenile court system, despite its mandate to rehabilitate, may not be able to treat certain serious offenders.

PROCEDURES FOR TRANSFER

The legal procedures and standards for transfer vary from state to state. The statutes or rules are often quite precise concerning the criteria to be used and the procedures to follow in making the waiver decision. If a psychiatrist is going to be asked to testify, she or he should know the specific laws in that jurisdiction. The court's legal office should be asked about the statutes that apply.

The eligibility of a juvenile for transfer is usually determined by the age of the juvenile and the nature of the offense (see Figure 10–1). The majority of the transfer statutes permit waiver only for older adolescents. Fifteen years is the most common cutoff age. The determining age is generally the age at the time of the offense. The ability to waive jurisdiction is limited normally to the more serious criminal offenses, such as felonies. However, some states permit waiver for any offense.

After eligibility to be waived is established, courts are then usually required to determine whether other factors, as designated by statute, are present before permitting the waiver to occur. Some juvenile codes have a general standard permitting transfer on a finding that the best interests of

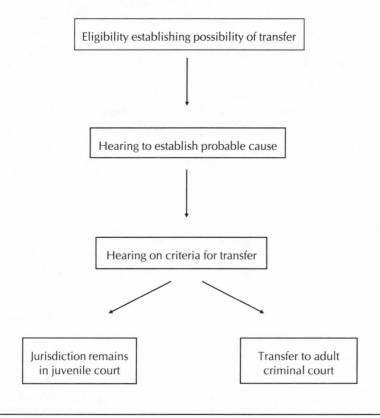

Figure 10–1.   Procedure to transfer juveniles to adult court

the minor or the public require it. Most states require more specific findings, often including criteria such as 1) the seriousness of the offense, 2) the prior record of the child, 3) the juvenile's response to prior treatment efforts, 4) the mental health of the youth, 5) the amenability of the child to treatment, and 6) the availability of appropriate treatment.

In the majority of states, the waiver process is governed by a judicial decision. However, since about 1975, there has been a shift toward two other models of the waiver process. One is legislative waiver, in which by law certain offenses or records of behaviors are marked by statutory exclusion from the jurisdiction of juvenile court. The second is prosecutorial waiver, in which the prosecuting attorney may file a charge against a juvenile directly in adult court. Florida, Nebraska, and Wyoming are governed by a prosecutorial waiver model.

The procedure for judicial transfer generally must involve two steps. First, the existence of probable cause that the offense occurred and that the youth under consideration committed the offense must be established. Next, the court must examine whether the criteria to mandate transfer have been established. Generally the most important evidence at a transfer hearing is the probation report and the mental health examination(s) of the youth. Mental health assessment of the youth is virtually always required, often by statute.

The burden of proof in a transfer proceeding is established by statute. In general the burden rests with the state because the juvenile code creates a presumption that minors of a certain age should be treated as juveniles. The standard of proof may be set forth in the statute as well. If the existing statute or rule does not specify a standard of proof, it is likely to be argued that the standard should be "clear and convincing" as recommended in the Juvenile Justice Standards (1).

The transfer hearing is a crucial stage of juvenile proceedings because it may remove from the minor all the protections of the juvenile justice system such as closed hearings, the possibility of sealed records, and rehabilitative dispositions. The importance of such proceedings is symbolized by the fact that the first juvenile court case to be heard by the Supreme Court concerned a transfer hearing, *Kent v. United States* (2).

THE PSYCHIATRIC REPORT ON TRANSFER

The psychiatric report should be a thorough presentation of the child's development, history, and clinical presentation. Particular attention should be directed at gathering clinical data 1) to establish the *Diagnostic and Statistical Manual of Mental Disorders, Third Edition, Revised* (DSM-III-R) diagnoses, if present; 2) to describe current service needs; 3) to describe previous interventions; 4) to detail the youth's use of, motivation during, and response to past interventions; and *5)* to discuss the minor's pattern of antisocial acts including chronicity, patterns of escalating violence, or specific precipitants to aggression. The data base gathered during the psychiatric evaluation should permit a discussion of the good and poor prognostic signs relevant to the treatability of specific disorders or behaviors present. Judges are divided about whether or not they wish the clinician to speak to the ultimate issue of waiver of the juvenile. Clinicians may also be in conflict about recommending what is perceived as a more punitive disposition. Whether or not the clinician speaks to this issue, the report must not fail to address all relevant clinical issues pertaining to treatability and dangerousness.

Treatment as a term relevant to the transfer proceeding should be viewed as a general term including not only mental health services, but also special education, work programs, family interventions, or placement. The court will be most interested in descriptions of needed treatment services and their relationship to future recidivism by the youth. However, the clinician should describe all identified needs and the expected degree of improvement, if possible. Treatment plans should be as specific as possible to permit the judge to decide whether such treatment is available and whether it can be carried out during the time the youth is under the jurisdiction of the juvenile system.

> Tommy, 15 years old, was before the court on a complaint of drug trafficking a small amount of cocaine and was referred for a psychiatric report concerning transfer to adult court. Tommy had a full-scale IQ of 75 and a long history of academic failure in mainstream classes. His involvement in the drug trade was as an occasional courier for older, brighter adolescents in the neighborhood. His grandparents, who were raising him, offered stable support and a willingness to participate in any rehabilitative program recommended. Tommy was assessed to be in need of a special education program and a schedule of structured after-school activities to avoid further involvement in the neighborhood drug trade. Evaluation showed no other evidence of antisocial behaviors. The evaluator went on to detail the available school and social programs in his community.

Although clinicians have more expertise in the general area of prognosis for treatment, the issue of future dangerousness must also be addressed in some way in transfer reports. A history of past violence appears to predict future violence, regardless of age. Age may be relevant because earlier onset of antisocial acts (before age 10 or 12 years) predicts future violence. Earlier onset is also related to the frequency and seriousness of later antisocial behavior. An extensive pattern of antisocial acts as a juvenile also appears to be a clinical predictor of continued antisocial acts. Transfer reports should address the number of different types of antisocial behaviors, the variety of situations in which antisocial behaviors occur (e.g., at home, school, community), and the types of victims. The reports also should address the frequency and seriousness of the antisocial behaviors, both of which are associated in the existing clinical research with patterns of continued antisocial behaviors (3). Newer work in the area of prediction of dangerousness also emphasizes the need for the clinician to analyze cognitive, affective, or situational factors involved in precipitating violence in the individual and the risk of the individual confronting similar situations in the future.

> Duayne, along with two other siblings, killed their severely abusive foster father. Duayne, the oldest at age 16 years, was referred for an independent psychiatric report concerning transfer. By history, clinical presentation, and testing, there was no evidence of an antisocial pattern of behavior or character traits. Duayne appeared to have a vulnerability to rage and violence toward sadistic, controlling men due to his past history of documented abuse at the hands of both his father and several of his mother's boyfriends. Duayne had a bright-average IQ, good verbal skills, and evidence of conflict concerning his actions and feelings. The psychiatric evaluation described Duayne as having a good prognosis if offered a therapeutically oriented residential placement and individual treatment with a woman therapist aimed at gaining cognitive and affective understanding of his issues. Duayne was not transferred to adult court and received the services as recommended. A 3-year follow-up showed no further aggression and a very good response to treatment.

The low accuracy of predictions of dangerousness, well documented in the research literature, is further impeded by the frequent encounter of denial on the part of the minor at the time of the waiver assessment. This denial may make a child look less treatable and more dangerous and is often encountered in the juvenile sex offender. Because a child is not found guilty or innocent until after the determination concerning transfer, denial of the allegations may be more related to pending legal issues than to personality traits. It is sometimes possible to distinguish this situational, conscious, and deliberate denial by assessing how much the minor relies on denial as a defense in areas not related to the specific offense.

The need to be clinically thorough and the need to assess denial emphasize the importance of using all available sources of information. These may include family interviews, school reports, reports of previous treatments, and probation and police reports. Both defense counsel and the prosecutor may be invited to submit any data for the clinician's review. As in all such forensic evaluations, the child and his or her family should be given an explanation of the purpose and scope of the evaluation as well as its lack of confidentiality (4).

A portion of the evaluation should be devoted to determining whether the adolescent is competent to stand trial in order to preserve the fairness and integrity of the legal proceedings if the youth should be tried as an adult (5). Competency to stand trial indicates the youth's ability both to assist in his or her own defense and to understand the legal proceedings. The evaluator should determine that the youth knows the complaints that she or he is facing and the role of the major courtroom personnel and is able to appreciate the adversarial nature of the legal proceedings. (See Chapter 5.) The youth should be cognitively, emotionally, and behaviorally able to cooperate with counsel in preparation of a defense. The evaluator should note whether or not the youth is able to give a coherent account of his or her actions at the time of the alleged event.

A section of the report should also indicate any mental health factors relevant to the offense. This section would note the apparent presence of a major mental illness or symptoms at the time of the offense and their impact on the adolescent's actions. Other details of the offense, however, should not be described due to the transfer hearing occurring before the actual adjudication of the case.

> Robert, age 17 years, was accused of stabbing a woman passing him by on the sidewalk. The psychiatric examination done for the transfer hearing described an adolescent with many schizotypal features. On the day of the alleged incident he was experiencing ideas of reference in which he believed the victim was laughing at his long trench coat and jewelry. This information was included in a section of the report entitled "Psychiatric Factors at the Time of the Alleged Offense."

Psychological testing is commonly ordered in a transfer evaluation. At a minimum, an intelligence screening instrument should be used (e.g., the short form of the Wechsler Intelligence Scale for Children—Revised). Personality testing may further substantiate the absence or presence of developing antisocial traits. Testing should be tailored to the individual case and to answer specific clinical questions.

Thorough waiver reports, summarizing clinical indicators for good or poor prognosis in relationship to treatment and dangerousness, are essential because of the critical nature of the waiver process. Once minors enter the criminal justice system, they are exposed to the same range of sanctions as adults. Research is divided as to whether or not transferred minors receive sentences that are more or less severe than they would have received in juvenile court (6). However, because 15 states have no specific age below which a minor cannot be transferred to criminal court by judicial waiver and several states have no crime restrictions before transfer is considered, many minors face transfer to adult court (7). The role of the forensic clinician should be to inform the court about the clinical issues relevant to amenability to treatment and dangerousness, as well as to inform the court of the limitations of individual predictions of future violence.

REFERENCES

1. American Bar Association and the Institute of Judicial Administration: Juvenile Justice Standards Relating to Transfer Between Courts. Cambridge, MA, Ballinger Press, 1980
2. Kent v United States, 383 US 541, 1966
3. Monahan J: The Clinical Prediction of Violent Behavior. Rockville, MD, U.S. Department of Health and Human Services, 1981
4. Barnum R: Clinical evaluation of juvenile delinquents facing transfer to adult court. J Am Acad Child Adolesc Psychiatry 26(6):922–925, 1987
5. Benedek EP: Waiver of juveniles to adult court, in Emerging Issues in Child Psychiatry and the Law. Edited by Schetky DH, Benedek EP. New York, Brunner/Mazel, 1985, pp 180–190
6. Hamparian DM, Estep LK, Muntean SM, et al: Youth in Adult Court: Between Two Worlds. Columbus, OH, Academy for Contemporary Problems, 1982
7. Shepherd RD: Transfer or waiver of jurisdiction. Criminal Justice 3(2):28, 1988

DRUG-INVOLVED ADOLESCENTS IN COURT

Richard A. Ratner, M.D.

The complex phenomenon we refer to as substance abuse has become a major social problem. In addition to the longstanding problems with alcohol and the opiates that had already existed in this country, the tumultuous changes of the 1960s and 1970s ushered in dramatic changes in usage patterns, types of drugs, and the way in which segments of society itself viewed drug use (1). Synthetic hallucinogens such as LSD made their appearance; the availability of marijuana became virtually universal; and there were some who predicted salvation through drug use rather than condemning the process.

To a greater or lesser degree, the seeking of altered states of consciousness through the ingestion of substances has always been with us. Our society has been of two minds about the acceptability of the use of any form of intoxicant, as evidenced by our history and current attitudes. Prohibition and its failure, the inconsistencies among different jurisdictions regarding the minimum age to be served liquor, and the rather popular but never successful movement to legalize marijuana are just a few of the signs of this ambivalence.

Thus drug use as a socially sanctioned recreational activity, at least for adults, has existed alongside drug use as an antisocial, self-destructive, and somewhat contagious social problem throughout most of our history. Although we are at a moment in our history when drug use is not being advocated as an agent of "mind expansion" or spiritual growth by any significant subgroup, we remain without a uniform national belief structure regarding drug use.

This lack of a national consensus regarding drug use is evidenced by the widely differing views about strategies for combating drug abuse. For example, a vocal minority of Americans believe that most drugs should simply be legalized and taxed as the surest way of driving the illicit suppliers and distributors of illegal drugs off the market. Others believe that the government should supply everything from sterile needles to the drugs themselves to individuals who are unable or unwilling to give up their use. One or more of these approaches are currently in use in other western societies (2).

Adolescents are particularly at risk for the development of drug problems. In addition to their susceptibility to many of the same factors that motivate drug abuse in adults, they are especially impressionable, risk prone, and exquisitely sensitive to confusion and inconsistencies in social attitudes. The testing of limits that is characteristic of adolescents as they undergo the process of separation and individuation may result in experimentation with drugs.

A large percentage of teenagers experiment with illicit drugs (3), but most do not go on to develop chronic problems of substance abuse. For many others, however, the experimentation leads to a more serious involvement with the drug or drugs, which in turn may result in court involvement.

In some cases, the presenting issue is ordinary criminal activity resulting from the sale, rather than the use, of illicit drugs. In others, use of drugs may lead to stealing to support a drug "habit," to violent behavior as a result of drug intoxication or psychosis, or to a variety of status offenses such as unmanageability or running away. A more recent development has been pregnant teenagers addicted to "crack" cocaine who do not seek prenatal care. At delivery, addicted newborns, many of whom are abandoned by their mothers, pose problems for the hospitals and the courts, which must find proper dispositions for both baby and mother.

The frequent association of substance abuse and delinquent behavior is well known. One study (4) found that over 50% of the teenagers sent to a residential treatment program for delinquency had a "noteworthy" problem with drugs or alcohol. This correlation of substance abuse with delinquent behavior has caused Peterson and Millman (5), among others, to conclude that "adolescent substance abuse is indicative of a general deviance syndrome that involves a broad range of norm-violating and illegal behaviors" (pp. 237–238).

CAUSES OF SUBSTANCE ABUSE

Substance abuse can best be understood as resulting from the interplay of biological, psychological, and social factors that are the roots of human behavior in general. Two major risk factors for the development of substance abuse problems in adolescence are social ones: belonging to a low socioeconomic class and coming from a family with a history of drug or alcohol problems.

For youths of lower socioeconomic status, drugs have a greater visibility in the community and are easy to procure. They also have a certain standing in the community because of the visible, if temporary, power and prestige of neighborhood and community drug lords. Further, the pursuit of sensate pleasure through drugs makes somewhat more sense to a person who perceives his or her alternatives as sharply limited or demarcated by racism, poverty, or personal handicaps.

Teenagers from homes in which substance abuse takes place are also at greater risk for developing the problem. Although considered a social risk factor, this statistic may also point to a biological role in causation.

Psychologically speaking, substance abuse may result from preexisting psychopathology. In one common scenario, a teenager self-medicates in an attempt to cope with intolerable feelings of anxiety, depression, or loneliness. Another pattern occurs when a seriously depressed teenager uses drugs as a type of Russian roulette. In other cases, a youth may use drugs to stave off an imminent descent into psychosis. It is not unheard of for drug users who are arrested to decompensate while awaiting release on bond.

Substance abuse that is felt to be "caused" by preexisting mental illness or emotional distress is sometimes referred to as "secondary." When no such predisposing factors are found, chemical dependency or abuse may become the "primary" diagnosis. In such cases, the dependency may lead to other psychiatric illnesses, including brief psychotic reactions, amotivational syndromes, or a wide variety of organic brain syndromes. Regardless of which diagnosis is primary, teenagers in whom both substance abuse and other mental illnesses coexist are now found in increasing numbers. Such individuals are typically described as "dual diagnosis" patients, and both inpatient and outpatient programs specially developed to deal with this population are appearing in facilities across the country.

per section

BEHAVIORAL EFFECTS OF SUBSTANCE USE

Bailey (6) classifies the known drugs of abuse into the major categories of "legal" and "illegal." Legal substances are further broken down into alcohol, nicotine, psychoactive medications, over-the-counter medications, and inhalants. Illegal drugs include marijuana, cocaine, hallucinogens, opioids, and heroin.

The effect of these different substances on the central nervous system and ultimately the behavior of an individual depends on a variety of factors, including the type of drug, the degree of maturity of the central nervous system, and the psychological status of the individual. It is well known, for example, that alcohol is disinhibiting; in an angry person, the disinhibition produced by alcohol may cause the person to strike out against others. Other drugs, such as the opioids, function as rather potent tranquilizers and are rarely responsible for violent behavior.

Alcohol is commonly implicated in violent behavior, as well as in such offenses as driving while intoxicated. Other drugs, such as the amphetamines and other stimulants, including cocaine, and hallucinogens such as phencyclidine (PCP), are also often present in the systems of teenagers arrested for violent behavior.

A review by Ratner (7) points out that current thinking about drug-induced violent behavior is centered on the effects of these substances on brain neurotransmitters. In common with certain other stressors, ingestion of amphetamines or alcohol leads to increased levels of the "excitatory" neurotransmitters, dopamine and norepinephrine.

In other cases, however, violent behavior may occur as the result of a psychosis that is secondary to drug use but that may manifest itself hours or days after the actual drug use has taken place. This delayed manifestation of psychosis has been particularly noted in patients who ingest amphetamines and hallucinogens, some of whom later develop a paranoid schizophrenic-like syndrome and require hospitalization.

Violence toward the self is also common. In some cases, if one is depressed to begin with, the use of drugs may trigger suicidal acting out on an impulsive basis. It is also not uncommon for drug-intoxicated individuals to harm themselves without suicidal or self-destructive intent. One individual was admitted to a hospital after ingesting PCP. While there he became delusional, thinking that "CIA agents" were out to get him and, thinking they were entering his room, threw himself out the window. In other cases, individuals responding to a psychotic grandiosity induced by certain drugs may jump from windows thinking they can fly or injure themselves in other ways while thinking they are indestructible.

ASSESSMENT

The psychiatrist's role in the assessment of the drug-involved teenager begins with the elucidation of the nature of the involvement. Perhaps the first question is whether in fact substances are being abused. Some teenagers are simply traffickers in illicit drugs whose involvement is for the money it may earn them, for the respect of their peer group, or in some cases, because of pressure from family members involved in the drug trade.

When substance abuse is documented, the psychiatric assessment must be aimed at sorting out the precise role that the substance use has played in the individual's life. The occasional situational use of beer or even marijuana, while not to be taken lightly, is different from situations in which drinking and driving, regular heroin use, or a psychological addiction to cocaine is found.

If the substance abuse is felt to be significant, perhaps the major question that must be answered is whether it is secondary to an underlying psychopathology, because this finding may help to determine what type of program is recommended at disposition. An individual who has underlying psychopathology may be poorly served by placement in a program designed to treat those for whom chemical dependency is the primary disease.

By the same token, past experience indicates that traditional psychotherapeutic treatment of individuals whose drug problems are, for whatever reason, primary will also result in repeated treatment failures. The misplacement of youths into programs that do not address their real needs is a significant cause of recidivism in both juvenile and adult courts.

The evaluation of the individual should be supplemented by a careful evaluation of the teenager's family to detect the role that it plays in the genesis of the substance abuse. For example, an adolescent's bouts of drinking may occur in the context of his or her entire family's regular abuse of alcohol. In a situation like this, a careful investigation might reveal no particular psychopathology, thus suggesting the greater influence of biological or social factors.

Families in which substance abuse is found may manifest other dysfunctional elements, including the presence of varying degrees of spousal and child abuse or neglect. In such cases, the teenage substance abuse may be a cry for help. The psychiatrist should be alert to these possibilities and be able to recommend further evaluation, if warranted. In such cases, recommendations may be made to the court to consider requiring the family to seek therapy as a family or, if this were to fail, to consider removing the teenager from such a home.

Similarly, the degree to which the youth is influenced by the neighborhood and subculture in which he or she lives must be assessed. This determination is also crucial to decisions about whether placement outside the community needs to be considered.

Drug abuse does not always reflect a treatable illness but may instead be a feature of an overall antisocial adjustment. If such individuals are unlikely to benefit from drug counseling or psychiatric treatment, it is important that this be recognized in order to prevent an unsuccessful course of expensive treatment. This type of misplacement is all too often used to support the argument that treatment "doesn't work" for anybody. Finally, the mental health professional has an obligation to himself or herself and to his or her patients to keep up-to-date in knowledge of the effects of substances, especially if he or she is treating adolescents. In addition, she or he must also be familiar with current treatment programs and strategies. This will allow the clinician to go beyond generalizations in making a recommendation and suggest actual programs that would be most beneficial to the juvenile, at least in the mental health sector.

Because drugs have become such a widespread and frightening public health problem, the public tends to think about the issue in black and white terms. Fear, anger, and a tendency to think punitively may overwhelm the judgment of the individual citizen and may even affect the deliberations of the courts in dealing with drug-involved offenders. For this reason, it is essential to make clear to the court exactly how a drug-involved teenager is involved, so that the youngster is neither punished when he or she should be treated nor treated at great expense and with little hope of success when he or she is not treatable.

REFERENCES

1. Rutter M, Giller H: Juvenile Delinquency. New York, Guilford, 1984
2. Rosenbaum M: Just Say What? An Alternative View on Solving America's Drug Problem. San Francisco, CA, National Council on Crime & Delinquency, 1989
3. National Institute on Drug Abuse: National Household Survey on Drug Abuse. Washington, DC, U.S. Department of Health and Human Services, 1989
4. Murray CA, Cox LA: Beyond Probation. Beverly Hills, CA, Sage, 1979
5. Peterson H, Millman R: Substance abuse among juveniles, in Juvenile Psychiatry and the Law. Edited by Rosner R, Schwartz H. New York, Plenum, 1989, pp 237–256
6. Bailey G: Current perspectives on substance abuse in youth. J Am Acad Child Adolesc Psychiatry 28(2):151–162, 1989
7. Ratner R: Biological causes of delinquency, in Juvenile Psychiatry and the Law. Edited by Rosner R, Schwartz H. New York, Plenum, 1989, pp 29–44

CHAPTER 12

PHYSICAL ABUSE

Kathleen M. Quinn, M.D.

Child abuse cases involving physical abuse come to juvenile court, frequently from child protective services, as complaints of abuse, motions for termination of parental rights, or cases involving unruly or delinquent complaints against older children. Physical abuse is defined generally as a medical condition of a child resulting from injuries inflicted by nonaccidental means. Many state statutes require a finding of "harm" or "danger of harm" as a result of intentional infliction of physical injury. Statutes calling for value judgments concerning the limits of acceptable physical punishment independent of a finding of harm or probable harm are the most difficult for the courts to apply. The near universality of corporal punishment as a disciplinary technique in American families and its relatively greater use in some social groups raise important issues of bias and arbitrariness in deciding what is abuse.

Although there is evidence that child abuse has existed from the earliest times, it first began to receive serious professional attention with the publication in 1962 of "The Battered-Child Syndrome" by C. Henry Kempe and colleagues (1). Today, there are 2.3 million reports annually of suspected abuse and neglect with an estimated 2,000 to 5,000 deaths each year. During the mid-1960s, all 50 states enacted mandatory reporting laws. Federal involvement with child abuse began with the enactment in 1974 of the Child Abuse Prevention Act, which established the National Center on Child Abuse and Neglect (2). There has been a dramatic increase in reporting of abuse and neglect since the enactment of mandatory reporting laws. It is difficult to know whether there also has been an increase in the actual incidence of abuse and neglect. However, very real increases have recently been seen in the number of children at risk for abuse and neglect due to parental substance abuse. At least 1 out of 10 children in the United States is born into a chemically dependent family.

The mental health professional is unlikely to be involved in the adjudicatory phase of the proceedings, which determines whether abuse has occurred. However, if a statute requires a finding of harm as an element of abuse or neglect, the clinician may be asked to determine whether a "mental injury" has occurred due to the abuse. In most cases at the time of the court-ordered psychiatric evaluation, a finding has been made at the adjudicatory hearing concerning the presence of abuse. The psychiatrist is called in to determine the psychiatric effects of the abuse, the treatability of the family, and the issue of risk for recidivism of the abuse at the dispositional phase of the proceedings. The psychiatrist is looked to for recommendations for services that will improve the parenting abilities of the adults and that will ensure the safety and welfare of the child.

ASSESSMENT OF THE CHILD

Although physical abuse may be the focus of the court's intervention, the forensic evaluator should keep in mind that any and all maltreatment may be present in either the child before the court or in the child's siblings. The assessment of the child before the court should include screening for conditions that make the child more vulnerable to abuse. These conditions include physical handicaps, mental retardation, prematurity, neurological damage, language deficits, and hyperactivity. Children with difficult temperaments may also be more vulnerable to abuse. The causal relationship, however, between abuse and development disabilities is most likely to exist in both directions—developmentally disabled children are more vulnerable to abuse by caretakers, and abuse and neglect may result in developmental disabilities.

The evaluator should attempt to understand the rules and routines of the child's home. Such a discussion leads naturally to an inquiry into what happens when the rules are broken or chores are left undone. The evaluator should ask specific questions about methods of punishment (e.g., what objects are used, what body parts are hit). Evidence of sadistic abuse (e.g., cigarette burns, starvation, torture) is associated with a poor prognosis.

An assessment of the child's emotional status is key to the recommendation of interventions and dispositions. An evaluation of attachments, through individual as well as conjoint sessions, is necessary for making recommendations for foster placement or permanent termination of parental rights.

> Inez, 13 years old, was seen alone and together with her mother and stepfather of 3 years. At the time of the court clinic evaluation, she was in shelter care after sustaining a severe beating from her stepfather with a hanger. She had a longstanding history of disruptive behaviors, fire setting as a preschooler, truancy, and suicide attempts. She vehemently wished to return home. Among the many issues to be addressed, the evaluator stated that this girl appeared unlikely to be able to tolerate a foster placement, which she would likely disrupt because of her positive attach-

ment to her family. She was initially placed in residential care while she and her family received intensive services.

Common negative emotions to be explored include guilt, fear, anger, depression, and self-destructiveness. A description of such affective states may be useful to treatment personnel seeking an initial focus.

ASSESSMENT OF THE PARENTS

The psychiatric findings concerning the parents are of crucial importance in recommending an appropriate disposition. It is the ability of the parents to change that is the ultimate key to protecting the children. Our knowledge of what constitutes effective treatment in some instances, however, is quite limited. In federally funded demonstration projects, recidivism occurred in at least one-third of abusive clients, and about one-third improved during treatment (3). The evaluator should consider a wide range of services, both traditional (therapy and case work) and nontraditional (parents' aides, Parents Anonymous, homemaker services, crisis nurseries, drop-in centers) when making recommendations.

At the outset, the goal of the clinical evaluation is to answer the following questions:

1. What are the parents' understanding of and feelings about the reasons they are before the court? What type of support systems does the family have? The parents' reaction to the assessment process is an example of their functioning under stress and their range of interactions with authority figures.
2. What are the parents' own histories of being parented? If the parents were mistreated as children, do they recognize those experiences as abusive and wish to learn other methods of coping?
3. What level of impulse control do the parents exercise? Impulsive behavior should be assessed in all areas of functioning, such as financial and sexual behaviors as well as aggression and violence.
4. How skilled are the parents in problem-solving? How capable of exercising reasonable judgment? Can deficits be remediated? How?
5. What is the quality of the parents' relationship with their children? This relationship should be assessed both through history and by observation. Parental values and beliefs regarding the children's needs and behaviors and appropriate disciplinary techniques should be elicited.

The final aim of the evaluation should be to describe the disciplinary techniques used by the family, their effects on the child(ren), and interventions that would best meet the needs of the family. A major problem for the clinician in providing an evaluation for the court is the focus, especially at the initial disposition hearing, on prediction. The state of the art leaves many unanswered questions about the reliability of assessment of past and present abuse, the poor record of intervention efforts, and gaps in knowledge about the effects of nontraditional interventions. Despite this, as "investigators" and "informed speculators" (4), mental health professionals can often contribute important information to assist the court in making a determination.

REFERENCES

1. Kempe CH, Silverman FN, Steele BF, et al: The battered-child syndrome. JAMA 181:17–24, 1962
2. Child Abuse Prevention Act (1974), 42 USCSS 5101-5106 et seq (1982) (as amended)
3. Helfer RE, Kempe CH: The Battered Child. Chicago, IL, University of Chicago Press, 1987, pp 152–177
4. Melton GB, Petrila J, Poythress NG, et al: Psychological Evaluations for the Courts. New York, Guilford, 1987

CHAPTER 13

CHILD SEXUAL ABUSE

Kathleen M. Quinn, M.D.

When confronted with an allegation of sexual abuse, the clinician is presented with a number of problems both in attempting to determine the validity of the complaint and in structuring the investigation and his or her own participation. Complaints of sexual abuse are difficult to evaluate in cases where physical findings are nonexistent or ambiguous, victims are difficult to interview because of their lack of communications skills, or the behavioral symptoms exhibited by the child could be easily attributed to other stresses such as divorce or behavioral disorders. Validation is also complicated by the high number of retractions and the inability of the very young victim to appreciate the abusive nature of the alleged acts.

The complexity of sexual abuse is matched by the complexity of the roles that the clinician may play in these cases. The clinician may be a therapist to whom the child discloses the alleged abuse or to whom a validated case is referred. Other roles may include investigator, evaluator of the child's competency to testify, or expert witness on the psychological aspects of abuse. Complaints of sexual abuse also raise multiple emotional issues for the professional involved. One must struggle with the urge to overzealously "protect" a child, feelings of anger and disgust at the perpetrator, or shock and disbelief. Management of these feelings is a major task for the clinician.

Child sexual abuse is any sexual activity with a child and is a crime in every state. However, there are numerous variances in laws from state to state. For example, the lower age at which children can consent to sexual activity varies from 11 to 17 years. In addition, the definition of prohibited acts varies from state to state.

Legal action concerning sexual abuse against a child may result in criminal prosecution against the perpetrator and/or a civil action in juvenile or family court. In the criminal justice system, the burden of proof is beyond a reasonable doubt, which is the highest standard. In juvenile court, an abuse finding may be based on evidence that is merely clear and convincing.

An initial important step before entering a sexual abuse case is to clarify one's role. Currently the majority of sexual abuse allegations are investigated initially by state protective service agencies and/or the police because of the mandatory reporting laws. Most mental health professionals, then, will encounter sexual abuse cases as referrals for second-opinion investigations, therapy referrals, or referrals for evaluation through juvenile court at the time of the dispositional hearing. Before accepting or beginning the case, it is crucial that the clinician gather information concerning the number and nature of past investigations, the status of any domestic relations litigation, and the actual goal of the referent seeking the evaluation. The clinician must be alert for referents seeking second, third, or fourth opinions concerning the allegation when an adequate investigation has already been performed. The initial telephone contact should also attempt to clarify the issues for evaluation so that the clinician can decide whether he or she is willing to accept the case and whether the referral is appropriate.

> Dr. K. received a call from a mother concerned about her two daughters' nightmares. Before making an initial appointment, Dr. K. briefly reviewed the history of the complaint only to discover that the mother dated the sleep disturbance to her girls' entry into a local preschool that was currently the subject of sexual abuse allegations. The mother's greatest concern was that the girls may have been sexually abused. Dr. K. advised the mother to report her suspicions to the local department of human services, which was interviewing the other alleged victims. Dr. K. offered to see the mother as soon as the investigatory interviews were completed if the girls remained symptomatic. She clarified for the mother that if indicated she could be available for a therapeutic intervention but would not reinterview the girls as an investigator.

Investigation should be clearly distinguished from therapy (1). Especially when the child is young, investigation and therapy should be done by separate individuals. The need for the strict separation of the roles is based on increasing examples of cases in which mixing roles has contaminated cases legally, compromising the ability to reach clinical as well as legal conclusions. This concern is so grave that in some states it is now a violation of the mental health professionals' code of ethics to do both therapy and investigation within any one case.

> Dr. R., a child psychiatry resident, was seeing a 6-year-old girl on intake for the chief complaint of overactivity. She was videotaping the session for review by her supervisor. During the session, the child stated that her father had touched her. Before eliciting further details, Dr. R. commented, "I'm sorry this awful thing happened to you." This and similar comments, as well as Dr. R.'s lack of structured interviewing techniques to obtain the

data, were later used to challenge the validity of the complaint. The prosecutor decided against taking the case to the grand jury because of these and other confounding factors after reviewing the tape.

THE INVESTIGATION

The psychiatrist who acts as an investigatory interviewer should be comfortable with the management of children and families, should be able to manage a wide range of children's behaviors, and should be experienced in interviewing children. Supervised experience in evaluating sexual abuse cases is most desirable. The clinician should possess knowledge about basic developmental principles, child witness issues, and child sexual abuse dynamics. For example, the evaluator should be knowledgeable about current findings on children's memory, suggestibility, and capacity to lie. These fields are changing rapidly, and the interviewer must remain current regarding the most recent information as it affects his or her interviewing techniques and interpretation of the responses of the child (2).

The primary goal of investigatory interviewing is to document the chronology, context, and consistency of the complaint. Care must be taken to keep the data as uncontaminated as possible. The investigation must be able to withstand the scrutiny of the judicial system and the attacks of defense attorneys who frequently attempt to demonstrate that the interview process itself has put words in the child's mouth. The investigation should reflect the child's experience, not the interviewer's assumptions or expectations. In order to achieve this goal of uncontaminated data, the investigator should adhere to two specific concepts: external and internal independence. In maintaining external independence, the evaluator does not ally himself or herself with any one side (3). In maintaining internal independence, the interviewer does not lead or influence the data that the child brings to the evaluation.

A record review of the local protective service agency indicated that in cases of intrafamilial abuse when a mother accused a father of sexual abuse, the workers saw the fathers in less that one-half of the cases. In addition to raising questions concerning the adequacy of the resulting data base, this discovery raised questions concerning the external independence of these assessments.

A local worker on a sexual abuse team stated on deposition that she had never seen either an unsubstantiated or a false allegation of sexual abuse. She maintained this position even when confronted with statistics that approximately 50% of all maltreatment cases are unsubstantiated nationwide and 3% to 8% are estimated to be false. She was subsequently viewed as seriously biased toward always finding abuse, and her investigations were discredited in the judicial system.

After intake, the evaluation consists of two major parts: history taking and the interview of the child. Every effort should be made to interview the alleged perpetrator. There are a number of psychosocial issues that must be clarified either at intake or during the parental interviews. Information should be gathered about the family's daily living habits (e.g., bathing, toileting, sleep practices, traditions concerning privacy and nudity, and their approach to sexuality and sex education). The child's exposure to sexually explicit materials and activities and the child's level of development concerning sexuality should also be understood. In cases of divorce or visitation or custody disputes, a chronology of escalating allegations should be documented in order to determine whether a pattern of repeated attempts to restrict the access of the noncustodial parent appears to exist.

A careful history of the child's symptoms should be obtained, and the occurrence of any other major stresses should be noted. The parental interviews should also include a thorough family history and child developmental history. It should be specifically ascertained whether the child or other family members have been sexually abused. Care should be taken to understand the details of these earlier victimizations and their impact on the individual. Particular care should be taken to note patterns of sexualization of relationships or unresolved posttraumatic stress disorder that may generate false allegations. Mental health histories should also be understood because psychopathology of the child and/or the parent may give rise to a false complaint. Prominent paranoid or histrionic traits in caretakers have been described in some cases that were assessed to be false.

The child should always be seen alone. This method is recommended in order to avoid undue influence by the parents. Even with the most supportive of parents, factors may contaminate the child's disclosure. A child may feel he or she must respond to a parent's expectation. Another may not want to reveal data in order not to hurt, embarrass, or anger a parent. When the parents are told the reasons for interviewing the child alone, the overwhelming majority become supportive of such independent interviews. Parents should also be informed that details from the child's interview will not be immediately released unless there is a need to protect the child. This method again attempts to minimize parental contamination. If the parent does not know what the child has said, the data are less likely to be viewed as altered by parental questioning. The child should be interviewed two to three times in order to assess the consistency of the complaints as well as to allow the child to feel comfortable enough to reveal sensitive secrets. Doing more than three interviews increases the chance of the child's feeling coerced into elaborating the story.

Each child should be interviewed by the same basic procedure. The environment should be quiet, private, and with a selected number of age-appropriate toys and materials. For example, for the preschool child these toys and materials might include markers and paper, play telephones (2), a doll house, and trucks and cars. Materials not appropriate for the evaluation of sexual abuse include sexual education and abuse prevention materials, puppets, or media materials related to the individual case (e.g., newspapers, photo lineups of suspected perpetrators).

There are two major portions of the interview: free play and structured questions. The goals of the free-play portion of the interview include 1) establishing rapport and 2) observing the child's developmental level. By noting the child's general level of abilities in the areas of cognition, speech and language, emotional development, and play skills, the evaluator is able to tailor subsequent portions of the interview to the individual child. The free-play period may last from several minutes to half an hour. The interviewer may move on when she or he knows the general level of abilities of the child, is able to communicate with the child, and has gotten the child to interact relatively freely.

The next part of the interview is a systematic evaluation concerning abuse. Tools to use may include the anatomically detailed dolls, the anatomically correct drawings, and the drawing materials. Numerous suggested interview protocols have been published (4–6); however, there is no research demonstrating the superiority of any particular protocol. Each investigator should choose or develop a protocol that is followed during each investigation. Such structured techniques permit the interviewer to learn the expectable responses of large groups of children, promote thoroughness of the evaluation, and appear to minimize leading and coercion in interviews. Initially, the child is asked for his or her names for both nongenital and genital body parts and the function of these body parts. The clinician should then begin with very general questions such as "Have you ever been hurt/touched on your body?" Then affirmative answers should be followed up with detailed questioning about the specific events and who said what to whom, the sequence of events, and any unique sensory experiences. The evaluator should attempt to gather data to distinguish, if possible, hygienic from abusive touching.

Thorough documentation of the child's interview is essential. This documentation is best achieved by videotaping when possible. Videotaping will preserve the child's initial statements, may avoid multiple investigations, and may encourage a defendant to plead guilty. Thorough documentation may also permit an assessment of possible brainwashing. However, there are also risks to videotaping, including harassment of the child on cross-examination and the issue of disposal of the tapes after the legal proceedings. Clinicians should familiarize themselves with their state laws relating to the admissibility of videotaped statements or testimony.

The interview of the alleged perpetrator as part of an investigation should address several areas. A thorough psychosocial evaluation should be reviewed with the alleged perpetrator both to compare various family members' accounts and to assess any significant differences if more than one household is included. A full psychosexual history should be obtained. This individual's past history of victimization and the content of his or her sexual fantasies are particularly relevant. The alleged perpetrator should be asked for his or her beliefs as to how this allegation arose. The evaluator may need to decide whether or not to observe the child with the alleged perpetrator. Such interaction should not be used to determine the veracity of the complaint. However, data from such a session may be helpful in determining the quality of relationship and the appropriate structure of any ongoing contact during the pendency of the case. The structuring of a treatment plan for the alleged offender is best left to clinicians specializing in treating offenders (7).

Occasionally the evaluator will encounter penile plethysmographic material as data in the case. The only appropriate use of the erection measurements in a forensic setting is as an element contributing to the expert opinion concerning potential treatment at the dispositional phase. A potential abuse of erection measurements in the legal context would be their use as evidence for adjudicatory purposes (8). Research demonstrating an individual's ability to voluntarily control the erection response strongly argues against the use of measurement of erection to "vindicate" an individual.

The polygraph may also be used in cases involving sexual abuse allegations. Clinicians must bear in mind that the polygraph is not a machine capable of detecting lies. Rather, it is equipment that records the autonomic arousal elicited by questions. Polygraphic questioning techniques have never been systematically studied to assess malingering or deception in a general clinical population. In addition, the administration and interpretation of polygraph tests lie outside the expertise of almost all mental health professionals. Therefore, the adequacy and competency of the exam cannot be assessed by the clinician. Deceptive conclusions have little probative value and should be given little weight (9). Truthful verdicts have more usefulness in the overall clinical evaluation. It is important that the polygraph be administered under adversarial circumstances and when the subject knows that the test results will be made public. The conditions ensure that there is a legitimate "fear of detection," a factor that has been held to be crucial to a valid test outcome.

After the completion of the evaluation, the investigator should produce a thorough report describing the nature of the allegation, the format of the evaluation, the content of the interviews, and an analysis of the clinical facts. Controversy exists about whether the clinician should state an opinion as to whether or not sexual abuse occurred. Whatever position the evaluator takes on this issue in a given case, the evaluator should remember that he or she merely provides clinical data to the protective services system and/or judicial system; the judge or jury makes the ultimate legal decision. The clinician should also address relevant dispositional issues for the child and indicated treatment issues for the child, alleged perpetrator, and family.

The assessment of the reliability of a complaint of sexual abuse remains a clinical judgment. Reliable complaints often, but not always, include a history of progression of sexual acts and verbal and/or physical coercion by the perpetrator. Some hallmarks of reliable complaints are descriptions of explicit, detailed sexual acts inconsistent with the child's baseline knowledge of sexuality. If the clinician can picture what occurred, the complaint is likely to be reliable. Credible complaints often include unique or idiosyncratic details given in age-approximate language. Although rating scales have recently been published purporting to distinguish real from false allegations, these instruments have not been validated by research.

> Lanette, 8 years old, alleged that her mother's boyfriend had repeatedly abused her. Her disclosure to the protective service worker included saying "Charles stuck his thing in my mouth. Then I'd taste something salty and sticky and feel sick." Her drawings and behavior were highly sexualized. She was hyperactive and a behavioral management problem in her current placement at her grandmother's home. She attempted to emphasize her story by giving specific dates on which the events allegedly occurred. The juvenile court psychiatrist saw this child for a mental health assessment. He decided not to reinterview the child concerning the abuse because of the adequacy of the mandated investigation. His report opinion concluded that "clinically, Lanette gives numerous indications consistent with sexual abuse. These included 1) an explicit and detailed description of a sex act not consistent with her overall sexual knowledge and experience; and 2) severely sexualized behaviors. Sexual acting out is the only consistently reported behavior in sexually abused children in both clinical and research studies. Her attempts to give varying dates appears to be motivated by her desire to make her story more believable to authorities and should not discredit the other content of the complaint."

Child sexual abuse must be reported in accord with the ethical and legal requirements of each state. Efforts at investigation should be coordinated with the mandated investigators (protective service and/or police).

Each child who may have been sexually abused should have a physical examination by a physician with special training in this area. The psychiatrist can perform a valuable role by advocating for a thorough and sensitive medical examination.

The possibility of false allegations should be considered, particularly if the allegation comes only from a parent or if there is a motive to lie (e.g., a custody or visitation dispute). In the rare cases in which a sexual abuse allegation is false, the major factor appears to be parental or child distortion or misperception of events. Lying is the least common etiology.

REFERENCES

1. Goldstein J, Freud A, Solnit A, et al: In the Best Interests of the Child. New York, Free Press, 1986
2. Quinn KM: The credibility of children's allegations of sexual abuse. Behavioral Sciences and the Law 6:181–200, 1988
3. White S, Quinn KM: Investigatory independence in child sexual abuse evaluations: conceptual considerations. Bull Am Acad Psychiatry Law 16:269–273, 1988
4. Friedman V, Morgan M: Interviewing Sexual Abuse Victims Using Anatomical Dolls: The Professional's Guidebook. Eugene, OR, Shamrock Press, 1985
5. Boat B, Everson M: Using Anatomical Dolls: Guidelines for Interviewing Young Children in Sexual Abuse Investigations. Chapel Hill, NC, University of North Carolina, 1986
6. White S, Strom G, Santilli G, et al: Clinical guidelines for interviewing young children with anatomically correct dolls (unpublished manuscript). Cleveland, OH, Case Western Reserve University School of Medicine, 1987
7. Sgroi SM (ed): Handbook of Clinical Intervention in Child Sexual Abuse. Lexington, MA, Heath, 1982
8. Travin S, Cullen K, Melella JT: The use and abuse of erection measurements: a forensic perspective. Bull Am Acad Psychiatry Law 16:235–250, 1988
9. Iacono WG, Patrick CJ: Assessing deception: polygraph techniques, in Clinical Assessment of Malingering and Deception. Edited by Rogers R. New York, Guilford, 1988, pp 205–234

JUVENILE SEX OFFENDERS

Kathleen M. Quinn, M.D.

The evaluation of sexual acting out in juveniles represents another challenging assessment. Questions such as what are "normal" or "acceptable" sexual behaviors, what is experimentation or exploration, or what is victimization may need to be addressed. The clinical assessment format will also need to be altered to include a thorough sexual history. In addition, countertransference issues such as inhibition about directly addressing sexual issues, voyeuristic tendencies, or repulsion and therapeutic nihilism may need to be monitored by evaluators embarking on such evaluations. A common reaction to juvenile sex offenders is often anger, disgust, or immediate labeling of the individual as conduct disordered.

Current data from victim reports and arrest statistics indicate that approximately 20% of all rapes and 30% of all child abuse cases, often fondling, involve adolescent offenders. Until recently, very little attention has been paid to these adolescent offenders for several reasons. Frequently, adolescent sexual offenses have been viewed by family members, treatment personnel, and the criminal justice system as sexual experimentation or curiosity. In addition, both the adolescent and his or her family deny or minimize the deviant sexual acts, making assessment difficult. Forensic practitioners are often asked to evaluate and to make recommendations concerning adolescent sex offenders. This chapter briefly discusses what is known about the juvenile sex offender and recommended assessment techniques.

Nearly all adolescent sex offenders are male. Girls account for less than 5% of all cases. Most victims of male adolescent sexual offenders are female. However, when the victim is a child, the proportion of boys is higher. For example, Groth found that 87% of peer or older victims of adolescent offenders were female, whereas only 69% of the child victims were female. The vast majority of child victims were acquaintances or relatives of the offender. Many of the incidents occurred in the victim's home during babysitting. Group rape appears to be more common among adolescents than among adult males. Sibling incest is believed to be the most common form of intrafamilial abuse (1).

Juvenile sex offenders commonly present with past and ongoing school and behavior problems. However, these disturbances are no more common in juvenile sex offenders than in other delinquent youths who have never committed a sexual offense. Approximately one-third of the offenders have no evidence of a conduct disorder. Compared with other male adolescents, the adolescent sex offender is more likely to have a history of being physically and sexually abused. Perpetrators who molest younger boys appear to have a particularly high incidence of having been sexually abused when they were younger.

Current research indicates that adolescent sex offenders claim to have more sexual experiences, including consenting ones, than do comparison groups of adolescents. This finding is in sharp contrast to the belief that sexual offenses stem from a lack of sexual experience. Recidivism rates and preliminary uncontrolled treatment outcome statistics are promising for the adolescent sexual offender, with recidivism rates of less than 10% in general. The recidivism rates in adolescent sex offenders appear to be lower than those in adult sex offenders. Clinically, adolescents are described as not reporting the frequency and intensity of deviant sexual fantasies that adult sex offenders do. In addition, the adolescents have fewer distorted beliefs regarding their deviant behavior compared with adult offenders (2).

Our current knowledge about juvenile sex offenders should inform our evaluation practices. For example, approximately 30% of adolescent sex offenders referred to an outpatient evaluation program totally deny their offense. It must be remembered that with offenders not fully disclosing their part in the alleged offense during predispositional statements, evaluation may be incomplete. The perpetrators' denial or minimization of the offense increases the importance of collateral sources, including victim statements, police reports, medical records, and social service investigations (3). These collateral sources permit an assessment of the degree of the minimization, lying, or denial, as well as permitting more effective confrontation of the adolescent. Collateral contacts with family members permit an assessment of their denial and of the family's sexual history and family structure. Gauging parental support for treatment is an important goal of the evaluation. In addition, family contact will permit a fuller understanding of any relevant family system issues.

The individual assessment of the alleged offender should include both a full evaluation of his sexual behavior and fantasy life and a detailed psychiatric evaluation. This assessment often requires several interviews. Exploration of the adolescent's sexual history is best incorporated into the medical history portion of the interview(s). Considerable time should be spent reassuring the adolescent of the routine nature of the questions given the allegations against him, as well as normalizing the existence of sexual thoughts. Sexual fantasies can be described as "a movie that plays in everyone's head." The adolescent can then be asked when he first experienced such fantasies and how their content evolved. Direct inquiry should be made about the full range of sexually deviant behaviors (including obscene telephone calls, voyeurism, exhibitionism, fetishism, etc.). Particular attention should be paid to evaluating the adolescent's current and past level of impulse control and aggression. A pattern of escalating violence and/or seriousness of the sexual offense is of particular concern. Sexual offenses involving violence toward the victim or a prior history of violence should cause the clinician to recommend evaluation and treatment in a residential setting. Other factors that may cause the clinician to recommend removal from the home include inadequate parental control, denial of the offender's problem, and the offender's victimization within his own home.

A full psychiatric evaluation should include a psychometric assessment of the offender's intelligence and cognitive abilities. Personality assessment with measures such as the Minnesota Multiphasic Personality Inventory (4), the Jesness Inventory (5), and/or projectives may be helpful in assessing the adolescent's personality structure. Testing, however, should never be used to establish that a juvenile is an offender. There is no validity to the use of offender profiles for such purposes. Other preexisting conditions such as learning disabilities, attention-deficit hyperactivity disorder, psychoses, or substance abuse should be described, and recommendations should be made for concurrent treatment.

When assessing juvenile sex offenders, numerous issues should be addressed in order to understand the resulting behaviors. The early history of the offender may reveal a pattern of socialization that includes dysfunctional thinking, antisocial behaviors, and exploitation (6). The family history may yield role reversals and patterns of denial and minimization. Most offenders' lives show a history of a lack of empathic care, resulting in a lack of empathy for their current victims. The role of arousal and fantasy must also be clarified. Situations that make the offender feel helpless or out of control often trigger the sexual assaults.

The court should be informed of low-risk and high-risk factors for reoffending (7). There are currently no validated instruments or criteria to assess the risk of reoffense. Clinical experience is the basis for current assessment decisions; therefore, caution must be exercised in representing the ability to predict risk. High-risk factors such as use of force, total denial in either offender or parents, compulsive deviant masturbatory fantasies, or psychoses are more powerful predictors than low-risk to moderate-risk factors (8).

> Charles, a 14-year-old boy, was seen after ejaculating on his sleeping mother and infant sister. A mental status examination showed that he was actively psychotic. He also revealed a compulsive fantasy involving the sadistic rape and ultimate murder of his victims. He was immediately hospitalized for his own and others' safety.

Recent research also demonstrates the existence of prepubescent and child offenders. Not all sexual activity between peers is abnormal or criminal. Whether or not this activity is considered problematic depends on the levels of equality and consent in the relationship or the presence of threats and coercion. If the relationship was exploitative or aggressive or threatened the physical or psychological well-being of either child, the behaviors are problematic, and specialized intervention may be indicated.

Not all referrals concerning apparent sexual offenses result in the clinical conclusion that an act was primarily sexual or that the individual is an offender. Care must be taken to not prematurely label a youth as a "perpetrator."

> Bob, a 14-year-old adolescent boy, was referred to the court clinic on a complaint of "sexual imposition" in which he was alleged to have touched a female classmate's breasts. Upon receiving all the materials on the case, the clinician learned that the two had had a previous fight when the boy had taunted the girl concerning her obesity. Several days later the two had encountered each other after school, and another fight broke out. The boy was sure that he had struck her in the chest area but was unsure if he had hit her breast. The clinician's report described this account, which was consistent with the victim's statement. The clinician indicated to the court that the act appeared aggressive and not overtly sexual in nature.

Treatment recommendations should specify sex-offender–specific treatment in a peer-based group, the most clinically efficacious modality. Exceptions to a referral to a group include offenders with language disorders, severe psychiatric conditions, or significant intellectual deficits. Adjunct treatments should be recommended on an individual basis.

REFERENCES

1. Groth AN: The adolescent sexual offender and his prey. International Journal of Offender Therapy and Comparative Criminology 21:249–254, 1977
2. Davis GE, Leitenberg H: Adolescent sex offenders. Psychol Bull 101:417–427, 1987

3. Becker JV, Kavoussi RJ: Diagnosis and treatment of juvenile sex offenders, in Juvenile Psychiatry and the Law. Edited by Rosner R, Schwartz HI. New York, Plenum, 1989, pp 133–143
4. Hathaway SR, McKinley JC: Minnesota Multiphasic Personality Inventory—2. Minneapolis, University of Minnesota, 1989
5. Jesness CA: The Jesness Inventory Manual. Palo Alto, CA, Consulting Psychologists Press, 1983
6. Groth AN, Loredo CM: Juvenile sex offenders: guidelines for assessment. International Journal of Offender Therapy and Comparative Criminology 25:31–39, 1981
7. State of Oregon Children's Services: Oregon Report on Juvenile Sex Offenders. Portland, OR, 1986
8. National Adolescent Perpetrator Network: Preliminary report from the National Task Force in Juvenile Sexual Offending. Juvenile and Family Court Journal 39:5–52, 1988

C H A P T E R   1 5

VIOLENT JUVENILES

Michael G. Kalogerakis, M.D.

Adolescents engaged in violent behavior have drawn considerable attention from government, the media, the juvenile justice system, and mental health agencies. The public has become increasingly alarmed with the succession of news reports of violent crimes committed by juveniles. The public's fear is paralleled by concern among professionals who have the responsibility of evaluating such youths and developing treatment programs that will meet their needs.

In 1984, out of a total of over 1,300,000 cases of delinquency and status offenses referred to juvenile courts in the United States, 61,400 or 4.7% were for index violent crimes (criminal homicide, forcible rape, robbery, and aggravated assault) (1). Another 5.6% were referred for simple assault, for a total of over 10% of all youths before the court for delinquency or status offense.

More recently, the Department of Justice reported that, between 1975 and 1989, the number of murders committed by juveniles tripled, the number of rapes doubled, and the number of robberies increased fivefold (2). The growth of drug abuse and in particular the advent of free-based cocaine or crack have led to a sharp increase in street violence, often gang related.

As the courts are being flooded with this population, it is becoming increasingly apparent that existing services for dealing with violent juveniles are woefully inadequate. This applies to legal and mental health services, and to both assessment and treatment. Many states have devoted particular attention to this group of delinquents, enacting legislation to process them in a different manner from the nonviolent offender, permitting automatic transfer to the criminal court without the formality of a waiver hearing, and, correspondingly, permitting more serious sentences (see, for example, the Juvenile Offender Law in New York). In 1989, the Supreme Court decided that even handicapped older juveniles who had committed serious violence could be given the death penalty (3).

In some instances, violent juveniles have been separated from all other delinquents at the point of placement, and special treatment programs have been devised for them, either in the juvenile justice system or in mental health facilities.

From the mental health perspective, there has been general recognition that it is appropriate to distinguish this group from other delinquents because they do differ in the seriousness of the threat they pose to society and in their treatment needs, although they appear not to differ etiologically or in their personality organization. In juvenile court, the psychiatrist asked to evaluate a violent youth is often required to respond to questions that may not normally be raised, notably, the potential for further violence or dangerousness. The importance placed on dispositional recommendations is proportionately greater, and the issue of treatability takes on special urgency.

The court is more likely to turn to the psychiatric expert in the case of a violent juvenile, particularly if the crime was homicide, than in most other cases that are adjudicated. The burden of providing reliable and useful input is never greater for the clinician. Although this may sometimes appear to be an unwarranted amount of responsibility, most forensic clinicians would agree that every violent youth deserves a thorough psychiatric assessment. Such an assessment will not necessarily prove critical in every case, but the prospect of serious deprivation of liberty, combined with the possibility of significant psychopathology, makes it essential that it be done.

DIAGNOSTIC CONSIDERATIONS

As with other special issues described, the standard assessment described in Chapter 6 must be modified to meet the specific requirements of this group, both as construed by the court and as defined by the clinician. Examples of assessment protocols for this population are available in the literature (4,5). This section will highlight some aspects of such evaluations, but the clinician who is called on to evaluate a violent juvenile is urged to refer to previously published material for a comprehensive outline of areas to be covered.

At the outset, it must be remembered that violent behavior and the individuals manifesting it differ greatly from one case to another (6). Violence may be individual or group, intrafamilial or involving persons unknown to one another, with the aid of a weapon or not. Street violence associated with robbery may have little in common with crimes of passion. The violent act may be committed by an individual under the influence of alcohol or drugs or by one who is sober. There may be a pattern of violence or a single unprecedented act. Some violent acts may be premeditated "atrocious crimes"; others may be understandable last resorts in very extenuating circumstances.

From the standpoint of diagnosis, violent juveniles may fall into any of a number of nosological entities as defined in the *Diagnostic and Statistical Manual of Mental Disorders, Third Edition, Revised* (DSM-III-R), including the following:

- Psychoses, which may be organic (e.g., amphetamine psychosis) or functional, especially schizophrenia and delusional (paranoid) disorder
- Conduct disorders, especially of the group or solitary aggressive types
- Mental retardation, usually mild or moderate, generally compounded by personality disorders
- Personality disorders, in particular antisocial, schizoid, paranoid, and borderline
- Sexual disorders, especially sexual sadism

Not all youths who commit a violent act enter the juvenile justice system. Much family violence—particularly among middle-class and well-to-do families and when the offender appears to be grossly psychotic—is more likely to come to the attention of mental health services (emergency rooms, crisis centers, a clinician in private practice) than the juvenile court.

In some respects, some of the differences among violent adolescents suggested above can constitute the basis for a typology. An example is the recent proposal by Benedek and Cornell (5) for a typology of juveniles who kill. Borrowing from previously published material, they utilized criteria drawn from the circumstances of the offense to classify their subjects into these distinct groups: *1)* a *psychotic* group, *2)* a *conflict* group, and *3)* a *crime* group. Based on a cohort of 72 adolescents charged with homicide who were examined at the Michigan Center for Forensic Psychiatry between 1977 and 1985, with a group of nonviolent delinquents as a control, the authors made a number of useful determinations, some of which conflict with commonly held beliefs or the findings of other investigators. Among these were the following (5):

- Psychotics constituted only 5% of the total sample.
- The prior record of delinquency was highest in the crime group.
- The crime group also had the highest rate of prior maladjustment in school and socially and the highest rate of drug and alcohol abuse.
- Victims of juveniles in the conflict group were usually family or close friends, whereas unknowns tended to be the victims of juveniles in the crime group.

- Weapons were much more likely to be used by the conflict group (where guns were a prominent choice) than the crime group.
- Three-fourths of the crime group were intoxicated at the time of the offense, compared to only one-third of the conflict group.
- None of those studied showed evidence of neurological dysfunction (7).

On evaluating the case of a violent juvenile referred by the court, the clinician should make certain to assess the following:

- The personality structure and biopsychosocial history of the youth
- The mental state of the youth at the time of the crime
- The nature of the relationship, if any, between the juvenile and the victim
- The dynamic interaction between victim and perpetrator at the time of the crime
- The existence in the juvenile or in the victim of "facilitating" factors such as drugs or alcohol
- The possible role of external factors such as third parties serving as *agents provocateurs*
- For those who appear psychotic, the possibility that symptoms are being faked (malingering)

The histories of violent individuals often reveal that they either witnessed family violence from an early age or were the victims of child abuse. Early signs of violent propensities may have been evident in the sadistic treatment of animals. Later, in some, a schizoid personality organization may have evolved, leading to isolation from peers and growing mistrust of the world. Others may have set off on a delinquent course even as preadolescents, gotten involved with a gang, or been propelled into violent activity by association with drug traffickers. A careful family history detailing violent activity on the part of other members of the immediate and extended family is essential, particularly for those who may have served as role models for the youth. In the absence of actual violence on the part of family members, family attitudes toward violence are potentially important and should be ascertained where possible.

Elements of the psychiatric examination that deserve particular attention include the following:

- A listing of all acts of violence admitted to by the youth and the circumstances surrounding them
- A careful review of how the juvenile deals with anger: what makes him or her angry, what his or her usual response is to being angry, whether the anger persists, etc.

- Associated fantasies: a detailed account of all fantasies and dreams dealing with anger, hostility, sadism, violence, and, for the sexually violent, sexual experiences
- For the psychotic, any violent or paranoid content of hallucinations or delusions
- Impulses of a destructive nature and the degree of control over them
- The quality of relationships to family members, to peers, and to other adults, especially the level of closeness and trust that has been established
- The juvenile's attitude toward the alleged violent crime and toward violence in general
- Feelings expressed toward the examiner, particularly if there is inexplicable hostility or belligerence

MALINGERING

The issue of malingering deserves special comment. Because the consequences of adjudication for a violent offense are potentially more serious (i.e., lengthy incarceration), the possibility that the juvenile will feign insanity is greater. Approximately 7% to 10% of a general forensic population are estimated to be malingerers (8). Figures are not available for juveniles, but they are likely to be lower (because of less experience in the criminal or juvenile justice system). However, the possibility of malingering warrants attention in every case of apparent psychosis.

Malingering adolescents tend to be brighter, system-wise, and more sociopathic. Less intelligent youths may attempt to feign psychosis, but their efforts are usually poorly conceived and executed. A skilled examiner should have little difficulty in exposing their often-transparent fabrications.

On the more difficult differentiations, a number of features in the history and presentation may be helpful. (See also Chapter 7 in this handbook, DSM-III-R, and Benedek and Cornell [5, p. 41].)

- *Affect and sensorium.* The true psychotic is more apt to evince fear and confusion; the malingerer's affect is unconvincing and often controlled or wooden.
- *Historical consistency.* There are two kinds of historical consistency: internal and temporal. Internal consistency means that the history provided by the youth makes sense clinically and holds together as a piece. Temporal consistency means that the story told in one interview is maintained essentially in the same form in subsequent interviews. Caution must be exercised because psychosis itself is often characterized by a changing clinical picture.

- *External confirmation of history.* Family and others (therapists, hospitals, schools, etc.) should be able to provide evidence supporting the juvenile's claim to have been mentally ill in the past and/or at the time of the crime.
- *Observation.* If the youth is in detention or hospitalized, reports of day-to-day behavior by staff may be the best indication of whether psychosis is actually present.
- *Therapeutic test.* Antipsychotic medication, which would normally be given to an adolescent in an acute psychotic state, should clear up symptoms such as hallucinations and delusions. The malingerer may not show the anticipated response.

DANGEROUSNESS

As noted earlier, the court's major interest in the forensic evaluation is with regard to the issues of competence, dangerousness, and concomitant treatment recommendations. Older adolescents committing homicide are frequently waived to adult criminal court and may therefore never be adjudicated as delinquents. The role of the clinician here will be essentially the same as that in cases not waived, except that the juvenile dispositions will not be available, limiting that part of the report. When adjudication has occurred, the treatment options recommended must be carefully considered and based solidly on the findings in the evaluation. Understandably, concern for the protection of the public will have more than the usual importance to the court, and the forensic examiner must bear that in mind.

The prediction of dangerousness and the psychiatrist's responsibilities in that regard have received considerable attention in recent years (9,10). It is entirely appropriate for the clinician to disclaim any expertise in predicting future violence in a youth who has been found to have committed violent acts in the past. Studies have demonstrated that the accuracy of such predictions, even when there is a long history of violence, leaves much to be desired, and because lengthy incarceration may be the upshot of such a prediction, defense lawyers are understandably very concerned about pessimistic statements by clinicians. At the same time, high-risk factors have been identified, and although much research remains to be done in this area, the clinician working with violent juveniles should be prepared to address the issue, caveats notwithstanding.

The best predictor of future violence appears to be a history of violent acts. If the recent history reveals a pattern of *escalating* violence (i.e., of more and more serious crimes), there is greater cause for concern, barring an unusual, effective intervention. The individual who seems firmly embarked on a life of crime, disclaims any concern for the life of others, and seems totally unmotivated to change is certainly a high-risk candidate for future violence. In the psychotic group, chronicity and unrelenting paranoid rage, particularly if past treatment efforts have failed, are worrisome features, but this picture is not often seen in adolescents.

The conflict group ultimately tends to have the best prognosis, assuming the intrapsychic and interpersonal issues that led to the violent actions are dealt with. Often, removal from the family setting in which the violence erupted is the most expedient remedy. However, unless the conflicts are addressed in individual and/or family therapy, no resolution of the problems and, therefore, no change in the ultimate prognosis can be expected. The exception is the occasional case of a youth who was never violent until he or she committed the one act that led to the appearance in court, an act that may be accompanied by a great discharge of pent-up emotion, followed by enormous relief and abatement of violent impulses.

The adolescent who threatens harm to others must be evaluated for homicidal risk. Adolescents who pose a significant risk to others must be contained, and any treatable conditions must be addressed. The range of options includes commitment to a civil mental hospital for the mentally ill delinquent or to a secure training school for the severely conduct-disordered youth. The prudent clinician will attempt to address both the relevant treatment recommendations for the youth and the aspects of a plan that will protect the community.

RECOMMENDATIONS AND TREATMENT

In spelling out recommendations, the clinician may be caught in a moral dilemma between what makes sense psychiatrically (e.g., training school) and feelings about the value of incarceration in the locally available facilities. It is sufficient in such cases to record what the needs of the juvenile are, for example, removal from a criminogenic environment, effective external controls where internal controls are clearly inadequate, an opportunity to organize his or her life academically or vocationally in a safe environment, or drug treatment for psychosis. The interpretation of how and where those needs might best be met can be left to the judge. In this way the clinician can preserve professional integrity while still serving the court and the youthful offender.

A Final Note on Treatment

Psychiatrists working in most juvenile courts seldom take on a treatment role, but an unintended benefit of the period of evaluation may be some therapeutic gain. Knowledge of treatment modalities and treatment settings is important if one's recommendations are to be of any value. For violent adolescents, the previously described treatment approach depends very much on the group they fall into. By and large, it may be assumed that treating the psychiatric illness that has been identified will have beneficial effects on the propensity to behave violently. Thus, a paranoid schizophrenic boy who is responding to command hallucinations that order him to kill may improve with antipsychotic medication and a supportive hospital milieu. Remission of the acute psychotic process will almost certainly end the homicidal preoccupations until the next episode.

The conflicts that beset the youths in the conflict group are not so quickly resolved. The period of institutionalization may need to be correspondingly longer, and the criteria for return to the community may be harder to establish.

Antisocial youths responded least well to therapeutic intervention. Because the violence committed is usually incidental to another crime such as robbery or drug dealing where a profit motive exists, the task of convincing the youth that his or her interests would be better served by giving up delinquent activity is difficult indeed. A change in values is required, which generally means a change in the youth's character structure. That is a long-term undertaking under the best of circumstances. If we add to this the poor motivation of such youths and the devastating impact of the environment they must return to, the necessity for extended placement becomes apparent. These clinical realities must, of course, be squared with the commitment to placement in the least restrictive environment for the shortest period of time permitted by the law. Such youths are generally remanded to the juvenile justice system, where the major rehabilitative efforts are educational and vocational, although mental health input may also be provided, commonly in the form of group therapy. Outcome studies have encountered serious methodological problems, but it is possible to say empirically that many of these youths seem to make adequate adjustments as adults, having outgrown their violent impulses. It is not known to what extent such improvements are developmentally related, rather than the result of treatment initiatives.

REFERENCES

1. U.S. Department of Justice: Juvenile Court Statistics, 1984. Washington, DC, Office of Juvenile Justice and Delinquency Prevention, 1987
2. A rising tide of violence leaves more youths in jail. The New York Times, July 2, 1990, p 4
3. Stanford v Kentucky, 87-5765, 1989; Thompson v Oklahoma, 101 L.Ed.2nd 702, 1988; Wilkins v Missouri, 87-6026, 1989

4. Lewis DO, Shanok SS, Pincus JH: Violent juvenile delinquents: psychiatric, neurological, psychological and base factors. J Am Acad Child Psychiatry 18:307–318, 1979
5. Benedek EP, Cornell DG: Juvenile Homicide. Washington, DC, American Psychiatric Press, 1989
6. Kalogerakis MG: The sources of individual violence, in Adolescent Psychiatry, Vol 3. Edited by Feinstein SC, Giovacchini PL. Chicago, IL, University of Chicago Press, 1974, pp 323–339
7. Benedek EP: Capital crimes and capital punishment in minors. Paper presented at the annual meeting of the American Psychiatric Association, New York, May 1990
8. Cornell DG, Hawk EL: Clinical presentation of malingerers diagnosed by experienced forensic examiners. Law and Human Behavior 13:375–383, 1989
9. American Psychiatric Association: Clinical Aspects of the Violent Individual (Task Force Report No 8). Washington, DC, American Psychiatric Association, 1974
10. Monahan J: The Clinical Prediction of Violent Behavior. Rockville, MD, U.S. Department of Health and Human Services, 1981

TERMINATION OF PARENTAL RIGHTS

Kathleen M. Quinn, M.D.
Sandra G. Nye, J.D., M.S.W.

When a parent abandons or severely and chronically neglects or abuses a child, the question arises as to whether parental rights should be terminated. This question may also arise when a parent is permanently and severely disabled. The issue of termination of parental rights comes to juvenile court after a finding of abuse, neglect, or dependency at the time of the dispositional hearing. In some states the question will be raised automatically if a child has been in foster care for a particular length of time. However, the more common procedure is for the question to be considered only if the state or some other interested party moves for termination of parental rights.

Psychiatrists have several possible roles in these cases. Psychiatrists may be involved at the time that a child has been found abused, neglected, or dependent and is also removed from his or her home. The psychiatrist would evaluate the child and the parents to assess parenting deficits and describe treatment goals to be incorporated in the proposed reunification plan. Psychiatrists can also be involved at the time of attempts at reunification or when termination has been proposed to evaluate the appropriateness of such interventions. Psychiatrists who perform evaluations in parental termination cases should know or obtain local statutes and case law because of state-to-state variation in conditions for termination.

Termination of parental rights may be one of the most difficult assessments performed by mental health professionals. The professional's participation in the decision presents numerous conflicts over basic values such as the maintenance of professional neutrality, tolerance for a wide range of life-styles, and the family's right to privacy and autonomy. Permanent severing of parental ties also acknowledges psychiatry's failure to treat or even influence many deviant parenting practices.

The current emphasis on permanency planning for children has made professionals increasingly mindful of the dilemma of foster care (drift). This emphasis on permanency is based on the belief that children need stability, continuity, and commitment from caregivers. The permanency doctrine also holds that children are best reared in families, not in institutions or by the state, and that the duration of placement should reflect the child's, not the adults', sense of time. The Adoption Assistance and Child Welfare Act of 1980 (PL 96-272) addressed many of these issues on the federal level, resulting in widespread state reform. When children cannot be returned to their own homes within a reasonable time, other permanent places are to be sought. The first step to achieve this goal is a determination of parental termination, freeing the child for adoption.

Termination itself occurs in a single proceeding in most states, although the proceeding is in two steps in some jurisdictions. In the bifurcated procedure, there is an initial "fact finding" proceeding to determine parental unfitness. The second hearing is to determine what disposition is in the best interest of the child. The legal standard for parental termination is often vague. Terms such as "unfit" or "unable to provide proper parental care" occur in the laws without elaboration. The vagueness of the standard permits wide judicial discretion. Concern over the risk of error has led to some reforms. One approach is to include in the proceedings a review of the adequacy of the services provided and the procedures followed by the state in the attempt to rehabilitate the parent(s). It is increasingly common to require a showing of "reasonable" efforts by the state to treat the parent(s). A second approach is to offer relatively narrow and objective standards to determine the need for termination. This second approach has been recommended in the Juvenile Justice Standards (1, pp. 111–122).

The burden of proof in parental termination cases is clear and convincing. This relatively high standard established in *Santosky v. Kramer* (2) recognizes the right of the family to remain intact until parental unfitness is proven.

The clinical focus of the mental health evaluation should be on the parents' competency as parents and the quality of the relationship between the parents and the child (and when relevant, between the child and the foster parents). Conclusions should not be based on diagnosis alone. The clinician must show the existence of a mental disorder, the parents' inability to parent, and the likelihood that the condition will persist over time regardless of treatment or services. It is the parents' level of functioning that is most relevant. In most cases both the child and the parents should be interviewed, and whenever possible, the parents and child should be observed together.

Ms. Diaz, a 30-year-old mother of six, was interviewed to assess her parenting deficits and strengths after her oldest daughter, Flora, 7 years old, had disclosed that her father had repeatedly had oral sex with her.

Each of the children was in placement. Several of the younger children had severe developmental delays and symptoms of failure to thrive. Ms. Diaz was overtly paranoid during the interview and vehemently denied the possibility that her daughter had been abused. She acknowledged no concerns over her children's status, stating that they were all fine. She saw no need for services. She refused to review any further history. A brief interactional session with the children demonstrated that only the oldest two children appeared to have any attachment to their mother. One year later the court re-referred Ms. Diaz. Although she was now more cooperative during the interview, she continued to demonstrate massive denial concerning her children's needs. She maintained her husband's innocence, although he was now incarcerated after being convicted of rape. Ms. Diaz had briefly participated in therapy and a Parents Anonymous group. She had left both when she was confronted about the abuse and neglect issues within the family.

The clinical assessment of the parents should attempt to address 1) the parents' ability to provide reasonable continuity of care, 2) the parents' capacity for empathy, 3) the quality of the parents' attachment to the child, 4) the parents' ability to organize and perform routine tasks of living for themselves and the child, 5) the parents' ability to seek out and utilize services and community supports, 6) the parents' appreciation of their child's developmental needs and/or special needs, 7) how detrimental the parents' behavior has been to the child, 8) the parents' ability to set appropriate limits, 9) the response of the parent to services offered, and 10) the limitation of effective treatments with certain disorders (e.g., personality disorders). The assessment of the child should address the child's developmental level and any special needs, the quality of the child's attachments to both parents as well as to substitute caregivers, the availability of a long-term surrogate parent, the child's adoptability, and the gains made by the child while in placement (3,4). Evaluators must understand clearly that the primary focus of the parental termination evaluation is on the capacity of the biological parents to parent, not on the child's best interest.

Collateral sources are often crucial to the understanding of these cases. By gathering documents from protective services and treatment services, the mental health professional chronicles the parents' responses to social service interventions as well as to educational and therapeutic approaches (5,6). Direct contact with workers and therapists often reveals additional information about the patient's motivation, attendance, and compliance with interventions. Such information permits better-informed treatment recommendations and conclusions about prognosis.

Numerous cautions must be raised about termination of parental rights. Clinicians should be careful to limit their opinions in maltreatment and parental termination cases. Available research gives little reason for

confidence in making clinical predictions concerning parenting capacity
(7). Equally sobering is the increasing recognition that termination of
parental rights and late adoption do not guarantee permanency for neglected or abused children who may resist or disrupt adoptive plans.

REFERENCES

1. Institute of Judicial Administration, American Bar Association: Standards for Juvenile Justice: Summary and Analysis, 2nd Edition. Cambridge, MA, Ballinger Press, 1982, pp 58–59, 111–122
2. Santosky v Kramer, 50 USLW 4333 (US, March 24, 1982)
3. Schetky D, Angell R, Morrison CV, et al: "Parents who fail," a study of
   51 cases of termination of parental rights. J Am Acad Child Adolesc
   Psychiatry 18:366–383, 1979
4. Schoettle UC: Termination of parental rights—ethical issues and role
   conflicts. J Am Acad Child Adolesc Psychiatry 23:629–632, 1984
5. Fialkov MJ: Fostering permanency of children in out-of-home care:
   psychological aspects. Bull Am Acad Psychiatry Law 16:343–357, 1988
6. Melton GB: Law and random events: the state of child mental health
   policy. Int J Law Psychiatry 10:81–90, 1987
7. Stewart D, Gangbar R: Psychiatric assessment of competency to care
   for a newborn. Can J Psychiatry 29:583–589, 1984

TRAINING PSYCHIATRISTS TO WORK IN THE JUVENILE JUSTICE SYSTEM

Kathleen M. Quinn, M.D.
Joseph J. Palombi, M.D.

The need for training more psychiatrists to do juvenile justice evaluations has been discussed since a 1975 survey by McDermott (1). This study revealed that many child psychiatrists believed that they were poorly equipped to do court evaluations or to testify in juvenile court. Today, many of these same issues continue for both adult and child psychiatrists. This chapter addresses the recent past, present, and future of training issues for psychiatrists in juvenile court.

THE PAST

The history of child forensic psychiatry is intertwined with the history of the juvenile court. The Juvenile Psychopathic Institute (later the Institute for Juvenile Research) was organized in 1909 and located within the newly founded Cook County Juvenile Court in Chicago. Headed by William Healy, the Institute for Juvenile Research became a laboratory for studying the individual delinquent, as well as a training site for mental health professionals interested in children, families, and juvenile justice.

Before 1972, there was no formal requirement for any training in either child or adult forensic psychiatry. By 1972, the guide for residency programs in psychiatry and neurology recommended experience in adult forensic psychiatry. Currently, the American Council of General Medical Education mandates a training experience in child forensics.

THE 1980s

The 1980s saw a burgeoning interest in child psychiatry and the law. In the area of juvenile justice, judicial, legislative, and diagnostic and treatment developments engendered considerable attention and debate. However, these developments were slow to be incorporated into residency programs for adult and child psychiatrists and into the continuing medical education for practicing clinicians or trainees in forensic psychiatry. For example, a 1983 survey of 130 child training programs conducted by Schetky and Benedek (2) revealed that of the 74 respondents, only 40 indicated that their programs devoted any didactic time to forensic child psychiatry. The average number of hours allotted to the whole topic of forensic child psychiatry was 5 hours per fellowship with a range of 2–10 didactic hours. In many programs, the child forensic psychiatry material was provided during the adult psychiatry years, not as a part of the child psychiatry fellowship. Only some of the programs provided experiential exposure to child forensics.

Project Future (3), a project of the American Academy of Child and Adolescent Psychiatry designed to develop a plan for training child psychiatrists in the upcoming decade, recommended that a limited number of child psychiatry training programs, research efforts, and continuing education programs be focused on juvenile justice issues. In addition, the final statement of the project suggested that all child psychiatrists receive training in the basics of forensic issues, including the psychiatric assessment of children and adolescents in both civil and juvenile justice proceedings. As important as these recommendations were, equally as important is the history of Project Future, which included the deletion of far-reaching proposals of the original task force, such as the development of training materials, a core curriculum, a core clinical experience, and regional training centers in child forensic psychiatry. Even the impact of the far more modest final proposal remains unknown. Project Future appears to have been a missed opportunity to increase training in juvenile justice issues.

THE PRESENT

Currently, the most available model for training in child forensic psychiatry is the mentor model (4). In such a model, the practicing child, adult, or forensic psychiatrist mentors with a recognized child forensic psychiatrist or a general psychiatrist who has an interest and expertise in child and family issues. The other model available for child forensic training is for a child psychiatrist to enter an adult forensic program that will tailor the training experience toward child issues and relevant placements and cases. In the late 1980s, there was only one program in the country specifically structured as a child forensic program. This program no longer exists.

The training issues presented by each educational track differ. For the child or adult psychiatrist placed in a forensic rotation, the first issues are desensitization to and immersion in the legal system. The child or adult psychiatrist must be oriented to the world of the court, its language, and its procedures. In addition, a child psychiatry trainee must be given ample supervision in the forensic interview. Such interviews, which are far more directed and focused than traditional child psychiatry evaluations, may appear foreign to the trainees. Another focus of the training experience will be report writing—teaching the trainee how to produce jargon-free reports concerning his or her observations and the relevant history. Assisting the trainee in writing opinions supported by data and relevant to the pending legal issue is another area of concern.

Clearly, all child and adolescent psychiatry training programs should offer an experience in child forensic psychiatry, including both didactic and experiential exposure to juvenile justice issues. The function of these experiences is threefold: 1) exposure and education in basic forensic issues and concepts; 2) training and supervised experience in the role of the psychiatrist in evaluation, report writing, and testimony within the juvenile justice system; and 3) possible recruitment of child psychiatrists for subspecialty training in child forensics. A model program would include, at minimum, a 3- to 4-month part-time rotation for second-year trainees with placement in a juvenile court clinic. Supervision is best provided by a recognized child forensic psychiatrist or a general forensic psychiatrist who has expertise in children's issues. Similarly, such an experience should be offered as an elective for adult trainees in their PGY-4 year. The forensic trainee will need considerable direction concerning relevant developmental, cognitive, dynamic, and family issues when evaluating cases. Relevant subspecialty literature needs to be shared with the trainee. The supervisor should both observe and critique the trainees' interviewing of the children or adolescents involved in cases.

At present, nearly 75% of all forensic fellowships in the United States and Canada offer their trainees diagnostic and treatment experiences with juveniles. The most common training format is a part-time rotation in a juvenile court clinic or juvenile detention center. The format and the amount of training depend on funding sources, affiliations, and interest of the faculty associated with each program. Presently, the Standards for Fellowship Programs in Forensic Psychiatry articulate general guidelines relevant to training in juvenile justice. The standards state that the clinical experience should include male and female adolescents, as well as cases involving child custody and termination of parental rights.

A major ethical issue for both trainee and supervisor will be the type of cases the trainee should undertake. The majority of custody and juvenile justice evaluations are performed currently by adult psychiatrists. However, debate remains as to whether or not individuals with only adult training should undertake custody evaluations without additional specialized training (5). Similarly, the age of a juvenile offender or victim or the nature of the offense may be a factor for consideration. Supervisors should counsel trainees on these matters, both before taking a case and when making recommendations for future practice. Psychiatrists who choose to do juvenile justice work should be aware of their limitations and know when to ask for additional supervision or consultation. For the child or adult psychiatrist, these limitations may revolve around the knowledge of legal issues and procedures. For the forensic or adult psychiatrist, the major weakness may be in the complex areas of child development and child interviewing.

THE FUTURE

Various forces may encourage or impede future development of training in juvenile justice issues. The pressing needs of the court system for expert testimony will serve as an impetus to the development of personnel with subspecialty expertise. The liaison between courts and training centers, including contracts for services, may benefit both. However, the continued aversion of many clinicians to forensic work will slow progress. Programs that lack an identified role model for training are also likely to lag behind.

In the future, two models may emerge. Benedek (6) has described the center of excellence in which a core faculty of forensic child psychiatrists will offer wide-ranging exposure to civil and juvenile justice child forensic issues for forensic trainees and practitioners. A second model, similar to the Project Future model, would have selected child psychiatry programs offer a concentration in child forensic issues within their 2-year program. Currently, the most realistic and practical model would be the concept of visiting lectureships in which recognized experts in juvenile justice and child forensics would travel to various training sites. Despite nearly 80 years of mental health input in juvenile court, we continue to struggle to make training and recruitment of psychiatrists in the court a priority. The challenge remains.

REFERENCES

1. McDermott JF Jr: Certification of the child psychiatrist. J Am Acad Child Psychiatry 14(2):196–203, 1975
2. Schetky D, Benedek EP (eds): Emerging Issues in Child Psychiatry and the Law. New York, Brunner/Mazel, 1985, p. xix
3. American Academy of Child Psychiatry: Child Psychiatry: A Plan for the Coming Decades. Washington, DC, American Academy of Child Psychiatry, 1983

4. Benedek EP: Forensic child psychiatry: an emerging subspecialty. Bull Am Acad Psychiatry Law 14:295–300, 1986
5. Goldzband MG, Schetky DH: Should adult psychiatrists be doing child custody evaluations. Bull Am Acad Psychiatry Law 14:361–366, 1986
6. Benedek EP: Forensic child psychiatry training. Paper presented at the annual meeting of the American Academy of Child Psychiatry, 1984

CHAPTER 18

PROFESSIONAL CONCERNS

Sandra G. Nye, J.D., M.S.W.

The psychiatrist working in the context of the juvenile justice system is involved in a complicated set of legal relationships. The law views the usual psychiatrist-patient relationship as a contract in which the psychiatrist owes a fiduciary duty of complete loyalty to the patient. The patient is entitled to assume and rely on the fact that the treating psychiatrist will act in the interest of the patient and not of some third party. The purpose of the contract is the rendering of clinical care for the benefit of the patient, who may be said to be the psychiatrist's client. When a psychiatrist is employed by a court to perform certain functions for the court's purposes, it is to the court that the psychiatrist owes a duty of loyalty. A psychiatrist hired by a family as an expert witness may find himself or herself in a difficult situation. Being part of an adversarial process means owing a duty of loyalty to the client and at the same time maintaining professional integrity.

This is not to say that the psychiatrist owes no legal duty to a child or family (let us designate them as the "court client") that he or she sees in the course of providing service to the court. Although a physician-patient relationship does not exist if the psychiatrist's activities are limited to evaluation and answering certain questions for the court, she or he does owe a duty to the court client to conduct the evaluation in the manner of a duly careful professional and to report the findings in an honest and objective manner. If, in the course of court-related employment, the psychiatrist renders clinical care and treatment to a court client, a treatment relationship arises that is legally complicated by the psychiatrist's forensic duty. Policies and procedures are required to delineate the psychiatrist's role and duty in this inherently conflictual position, and the patient and his or her parent must be clearly informed of the nature and parameters of the clinical relationship, including confidentiality.

DEFINING THE ROLE AND FUNCTIONS
OF CLINICAL PERSONNEL IN THE COURT

The court is responsible for organizing its clinical services program in a workable manner. It is difficult, if not impossible, for a court psychiatrist to operate effectively without policies and procedures establishing his or her role, the roles of other court personnel, and how he or she relates to these other court personnel. Is the psychiatrist responsible for physical examinations? Is the clinician responsible only for the psychiatric examination of the child or for the psychosocial evaluation of the family as well? Who is responsible for taking histories, obtaining consents, obtaining records of prior treatment, verifying facts, interviewing collaterals, and being in contact with the child's school? Who is responsible for locating, evaluating, and contracting with community resources for potential referrals? Who is responsible for making referrals operational and for follow-up? What is the psychiatrist's role in each of these functions? Is the psychiatrist responsible for control or supervision of other court clinical personnel? If so, what liability protections are in place for him or her? Who is the court psychiatrist's legal advisor?

THE CONTRACT WITH THE COURT

The psychiatrist should understand clearly the parameters of his or her contract with the court. A written contract is recommended (see Appendix 6), and the following issues should be addressed:

- *Term.* When does the contract begin and end? Under what conditions can it be terminated before the end of the term? What are the conditions of extension or renewal?
- *Time.* How many hours per week or month is the doctor obliged to give the court? How many hours per week or month is the court obliged to employ the doctor? When is service to be provided?
- *Duties.* What functions is the psychiatrist to perform? Is he or she responsible for physical examinations? Taking individual and/or family histories? Obtaining records of past treatment? Getting releases for those records? Doing psychosocial evaluation of the family? Verifying facts, as in interviews with school personnel and home visits? What other clinical personnel are employed by the court, and how may the psychiatrist gain access to their information?
- *Remuneration.* Is the doctor a salaried employee or an independent contractor? Are there benefits? How much is to be paid, and when?

- *Work conditions.* Where are services to be performed? What are the arrangements for office space, utilities, supplies, and support, and who pays for them? Who is responsible for premises and equipment liability?
- *Immunity.* Does the juvenile court statute grant immunity and/or indemnification to the doctor from liability arising out of his or her court activities? If so, what are the conditions of the immunity?
- *Malpractice insurance.* Is the doctor responsible for carrying malpractice insurance, or does the court insure the doctor? What are the limits and conditions of the insurance called for?
- *Confidentiality.* What is the doctor obliged to reveal to the court? To the parents? Is there a privilege for information *not* related to the instant proceeding? If the doctor discovers reportable facts hitherto unknown to the authorities, is she or he obligated to report them or forbidden by statute from doing so? (This may be covered by statute but should be stated separately in the contract and court policies as well.)
- *Conflicts of interest.* What, if any, restrictions are there on the doctor accepting a court client for treatment? Is the doctor restricted in referring court clients? Do the restrictions survive the contract and/or the court proceeding? If so, for how long?

COURT-ORDERED EVALUATIONS

If the court has not developed a referral form, the psychiatrist should do so. Whether the psychiatrist is hired by the court or by a litigant, every referral for evaluation should indicate precisely what the role of the psychiatrist is in the case, i.e., the nature of the information sought by the court and the use to which it will be put. For example, early in the process of a case, the court may wish to know the child's mental state and family circumstances to aid in determining whether he or she is to be detained pending further proceedings. If detention is indicated, what should the conditions be? The court may further inquire as to the child's fitness to stand trial, as fitness is defined in the local statute. Is the child psychotic, retarded, or otherwise physically or mentally impaired? Is immediate placement or referral for treatment necessary either for the child's best interests or for the safety of others? In the adjudication phase of the case, if a "not guilty by reason of insanity" defense is available in the jurisdiction, the court may want an evaluation of the child's sanity at the time that the delinquent act was committed. In the dispositional phase, the court will wish to know the child's clinical condition, needs and prognosis, and family and other resources and will want the psychiatrist to make a recommendation.

INFORMED CONSENT IN COURT-ORDERED EVALUATIONS

Before the psychiatrist commences an evaluation of a court client, child or adult, the client must be fully informed, orally and in writing, of the nature of the evaluation, the purpose for which the information elicited will be used, and the parameters of confidentiality. A written information statement should be provided to the client and his or her parent and attorney, and written consents should be obtained in accordance with local law. If the interview is audiotaped or videotaped, it is a good idea to tape the consent procedure. Some jurisdictions permit the court client's attorney to be present during the evaluation, in which event a preinterview conference with the attorney may be indicated to inform him or her about the process and reduce the risk of disruption or contamination of the examination. Some jurisdictions, however, do not permit the court client's attorney to be present during the evaluation.

Records of any prior treatment should be obtained. For the court psychiatrist, court policies and procedures will determine who is responsible for obtaining consent from the court clients for release of the records to the evaluator. Statute, court policy, and parental consent should determine to whom and for what purpose the evaluator may redisclose those records. If there are no statutory or policy guidelines, the evaluator should seek a legal opinion from the court's legal officer or, if necessary, from his or her own attorney and instigate the development of a policy.

AVOIDING CONFLICTS OF INTEREST

It is not uncommon for a family to seek ongoing treatment services on a private basis either while the court proceedings are pending or after their conclusion. It is recommended that the court psychiatrist avoid any private relationship with a court client or his or her family during the pendency of the case. To do otherwise will put the doctor in an irreconcilable conflict of interest between his or her role as a court functionary and his or her role as a treatment provider; a treatment relationship imposes a fiduciary duty to the patient that cannot help but conflict with the doctor's duty to the court. In a private practice situation, the psychiatrist should consider carefully the complications for treatment if he or she assumes both forensic and treatment roles for the same client.

Even after the court proceeding concludes, the court psychiatrist should think twice about the ramifications of undertaking treatment of a court client or family, although court policy may not forbid it. If the court client comes to the attention of the court again or a sibling becomes involved with the court, the court psychiatrist will find himself or herself compromised. In the event that the court psychiatrist does undertake a treatment relationship, the matter of conflict of interest must be discussed with both the family and the court, and it is wise to have a written statement from both setting forth the conditions of the relationship.

PROFESSIONAL LIABILITY RISK
FOR THE PSYCHIATRIST-EVALUATOR

The duty of the psychiatrist-evaluator to the persons being evaluated is limited to conducting the evaluation in accordance with the standard of good psychiatric practice and making the report and recommendations in a fair, reasonable, and objective manner. The standard of practice for a psychiatric examination in the context of a court evaluation is the same as that in any other setting. In a treatment context, there might be instances in which the psychiatrist will elect to forego obtaining records of previous treatment. In the context of a court evaluation, scrupulous attention should be paid to collecting all relevant clinical data as the basis for a report and recommendation.

The court psychiatrist may find himself or herself confronted with a dilemma when it comes to treatment or placement recommendations. It is not unusual for a court to explicitly or implicitly instruct its psychiatrist to make treatment or placement recommendations consistent with local budgetary exigencies and resource availability. When the child's needs are inconsistent with the court's financial abilities, a conflict of interest may exist for the psychiatrist. The court's expectations in this direction should be clearly ascertained at the outset so that the psychiatrist can make an informed choice as to whether she or he can ethically work in the system.

It is recommended that the diagnosis, report, and recommendations be made without clinical compromises. The child's actual condition and needs should be honestly stated, and if reality requires, any fallback recommendation should be labeled as the best alternative among available resources. A less-than-honest report and recommendation will expose the psychiatrist to risk of an accusation of substandard professional conduct, a complaint to the licensing authorities and professional ethics board, and a lawsuit. So long as the evaluating psychiatrist is not negligent in conducting the examination and the report and recommendations meet the standard of practice in the community, the risk of a malpractice suit is no greater than that in other areas of practice, and perhaps less.

LIABILITY FOR REFERRALS

A psychiatrist is not liable for the negligence or wrongful conduct of a professional or program to whom the youth was referred, so long as the referral is not negligent and the psychiatrist does not control the services to be rendered. Before making a referral to another professional or program, the doctor is well advised to check credentials and references. Of particular relevance are academic credentials, licensure, and malpractice insurance. If doubt exists about a particular professional or facility, it may be wise to refer the youth to another resource. It is unethical, illegal, and a breach of duty to the court and the court client to accept a commission, forwarding fee or percentage, or any other remuneration for a referral.

CONFIDENTIALITY, PRIVACY, AND PRIVILEGE IN THE COURT CONTEST

The terms *confidentiality, privacy,* and *privilege* are often used interchangeably by both lawyers and clinicians and thus become the source of much confusion. These concepts are related but different.

Privacy

Privacy is the right of an individual to 1) be left alone, i.e., free of intrusion on his or her seclusion and of unwarranted governmental interference with one's body and personal decision making; 2) to control the use of his or her name and likeness; and 3) not to have private, confidential information disclosed to anyone who does not have a legitimate interest in receiving it. There is a constitutional right of privacy that applies to government action only. The constitutional right to privacy is not specifically enunciated in the Constitution but is a principle derived by the Supreme Court from the "penumbra" surrounding enunciated rights. There is a private right of privacy as well, the breach of which is an intentional wrongful act and can be the basis of a lawsuit against the tort-feasor (the person who commits the tort or wrongful act).

Although a court client does not have the same confidentiality rights as a patient, she or he does have whatever confidentiality rights are provided by juvenile court statute and regulations. Usually, juvenile court acts mandate and define the parameters of confidentiality. The court client also has privacy rights. The court psychiatrist (and other court personnel) may not disclose private information about a court client or family except as authorized by the client or family or by the court. Violation of the juvenile court act is a crime; breach of a client's privacy is actionable.

Confidentiality

Confidentiality is the legal and ethical duty of a psychiatrist not to disclose information obtained in the course of evaluating or treating a patient unless the client has given informed consent, except as the law otherwise requires or permits. The duty of confidentiality arises out of the physician-patient contractual relationship and is an element of the fiduciary duty of the psychiatrist to a patient. If the psychiatrist's contract is with the court for evaluation, and not with the court client for treatment, the duty of confidentiality will be determined by court and statutory parameters and will be different from that of the treatment relationship. Put another way, the duty of confidentiality is different for the treating psychiatrist than for the nontreating evaluator; the right of confidentiality of a patient is different from that of a nonpatient subject of an evaluation for nontreatment purposes.

Privilege

Privilege, in the context of privacy and confidentiality, is short for testimonial privilege, a statutorily created rule of evidence that permits the holder to prevent the person to whom confidential information was given from disclosing it in a judicial, administrative, or legislative proceeding in which testimony or production of documents could otherwise be compelled. (The word *privilege* has other meanings in forensic psychiatry. Note the context to ascertain the manner in which the word is being used. See the Glossary.)

Many state statutes create a testimonial privilege for information obtained in the course of psychiatric treatment, consultation, or evaluation for treatment purposes. An essential element of privilege is that the giver of information has an expectation that it will not be disclosed. When a court client is under court order for evaluation, there is no such expectation. Therefore, and usually by express statutory provision, there is no privilege as to information obtained in a court-ordered evaluation, at least as to facts and circumstances surrounding the case for which the evaluation is being done. Some jurisdictions stipulate that the subject must have been informed of the absence of confidentiality or the evaluation will be excluded. In some states, although there may be a general privilege for psychiatric information, it does not apply in juvenile court cases at all. There may be other exceptions, such as child abuse and neglect or homicide cases.

Privilege law is extremely complex and will always be strictly and narrowly construed by the courts. Courts do not like privileges because they shield information that is needed for the court to do its work. The court will try to find *no* privilege, if it can, so a treating or consulting psychiatrist whose patient is involved in any court proceeding should seek legal consultation as early as possible. Most states' laws do not extend privilege to couple, family, or group therapy and hold that privilege is "polluted" by any sharing or disclosure of information, even accidentally, or by way of an unknown listener or eavesdropper (a clinical supervisor? insurance auditor? utilization reviewer?). Local law varies widely, and a knowledgeable lawyer is a necessary consultant for any psychiatric practice that has minimal forensic contacts.

CONCLUDING REMARKS
AND FUTURE PERSPECTIVES

Michael G. Kalogerakis, M.D.

From the first, this handbook was conceived and written as a practical guide for the practitioner. Though psychiatrists work in all aspects of the juvenile justice system, it was felt that the work performed in relationship to the juvenile court was clearly the most important as well as the most complex. The decision to limit ourselves to court operations automatically eliminated consideration of treatment methods from our agenda because very little treatment is done in the courts themselves. On the other hand, the decision involved the authors in the legal process and in the issues of interacting with it. The presence of a juvenile court judge, a lawyer, and a social worker on the workgroup served to educate and stimulate the rest of us from the mental health field, particularly because much of the planning and editing took place during the many hours that the group spent in face-to-face deliberation and inquiry.

With the stated purpose clearly in mind, we have avoided writing a primer on juvenile delinquency. Although we are all fervent child advocates, we have eschewed all but the most unavoidable advocacy positions. In these closing comments, however, we turn our attention briefly to two absolutely basic concerns: the viability of the juvenile court and the relevance of mental health expertise to that court's operations.

Television serials notwithstanding, the courtroom is not always the scene of an exciting, intense human drama. It is more often the site of a rather routine unfolding of well-choreographed performances by the principal participants with outcomes that are quite predictable. Perhaps because of the youth of their subjects and the problems they deal with, the juvenile and family courts are often the scene of pathos and despair. None who work in that setting can long escape the heartrending experience of seeing close up families in the throes of disintegration and children spiralling downhill, caught in a vortex of social and psychological forces beyond their control.

As the juvenile court nears the centenary of its birth, this much-maligned institution struggles to justify its existence and to serve needy families and society. Despite having undergone fundamental changes in response to criticisms of the past quarter century, the juvenile court continues to be attacked from the left and from the right. The civil libertarians focus on the issues of due process and seek to extend the gains begun by *Kent* and *Gault* in the late 1960s. Those of a more conservative bent are convinced that the court should pursue a punishment model, more in keeping with adult criminal court. Both groups have long been disenchanted with the rehabilitation philosophy that gave rise to the court in the first place. Thus, Whitebread and Heilman, in their fine overview of the law of juvenile delinquency, state that "the major issue facing the juvenile justice system is whether the rehabilitative role has failed to fulfill its objective" (1, p. 305). These authors express their belief that the attacks on the rehabilitative ideal will continue in the years ahead: ". . . [I]f the history of delinquency law is any indication, the tension in the juvenile justice system between rehabilitation and punishment will never be conclusively resolved" (1, p. 305).

There is little reason to fear that the juvenile court will meet its demise in the near or distant future, although, like all of society's institutions, it must continue to adapt to the changing times. Its functions are too specialized to be reassigned to any other court. It must be remembered that the juvenile court is but one cog in the wheel that is the juvenile justice and child care system. The effect on the overall system of eliminating the juvenile court is hard to imagine but would in all probability be chaos.

Whatever its shortcomings, the juvenile court continues to provide the unique services for which it was designed. There are a number of compelling reasons for retaining the juvenile court essentially in its present form:

- Not all juvenile delinquents are hard-core cases beyond rehabilitation; many are treatable youngsters swept along by neighborhood forces they cannot resist.
- Status offenders, still handled by juvenile court in many jurisdictions, are not criminals.
- Abuse and neglect cases, which make up a large part of the juvenile court calendar, can only be handled by a court prepared to deal with dysfunctional families as a whole and in a therapeutic atmosphere (although there are states where adult courts perform this function).
- The child care system, which includes education, child welfare, juvenile justice, and child mental health, would not assume responsibility for the products of the adult criminal system.

- "Just deserts," proportionality, and determinate sentencing are already available in the juvenile system, notably via the mechanism of waiver for felonious delinquents.
- The "unbridled" discretionary power of judges has been curbed both by legislation and increased effectiveness of legal representation.
- Some of the failings of the juvenile justice system are failings of the care and treatment sector, not the juvenile court (e.g., premature discharge, no follow-up programs).
- In its limit-setting powers and ability to enforce cooperation by recalcitrant families, the juvenile court serves an important therapeutic role.
- Both adult and juvenile systems have failed to achieve desired results with hard-core, antisocial offenders.
- Finally, some states (e.g., New York) have enacted legislation that makes it possible to keep the more dangerous offenders under lock and key for years, thus nullifying what some maintain is the "advantage" of the adult criminal system.

Not only the juvenile court has been under attack. Both the need for and value of mental health experts in the juvenile court have been questioned. It is apparent that, for the foreseeable future, mental health professionals will remain vulnerable to accusations of representing an imperfect science, being handicapped by ever-changing diagnostic categories and criteria, extrapolating too readily from limited data to arrive at conclusions having dubious validity and reliability, being too quick to predict when available studies cast serious doubt on the reliability of clinical prognostication, engaging in omnipotent flights of fancy when making dispositional recommendations, and so forth. It must be recognized that many of these criticisms are derived from actual experience in the courtroom. What is not often noted is that they also describe the failings of the incompetent or inexperienced practitioner, not those of a profession whose unique contributions to society are well established and evident in many areas.

Improving levels of competence among clinicians serving the court will redound to the benefit of all. The same can be said for judges, lawyers, probation officers, and other juvenile court personnel. It is this principle that led to the writing of this handbook and dictates the emphasis the authors have placed on adequate training.

On the other hand, apart from considerations of performance level, there was unanimity among the contributors that the role of mental health services in the court is vital and the forensic clinician is irreplaceable. As long as some youths who commit delinquent acts are mentally ill or emotionally disturbed, as long as some delinquency is causally related to one's mental state or psychiatric history, as long as competency issues and the insanity defense remain a part of American jurisprudence, as long as youngsters who come before the court are victims of unstable, disturbed parenting (not only in cases of flagrant abuse), and as long as the court needs to have assessments of treatability of youths or their parents, the mental health professional will remain a valuable, integral member of the juvenile court team. Who else can provide the expertise in the mental health area demanded by the court? Who but the forensic clinician can represent the biopsychosocial perspective that may be indispensable to a proper finding or a carefully crafted disposition?

In a useful review of the critiques of mental health expertise in juvenile law, Aber and Repucci (2) argue for full disclosure by the expert of the basis for opinions and conclusions provided to the court. The authors of this handbook are in full agreement with such a policy and have so indicated in various chapters throughout the book. There is no reason why a well-reasoned opinion should not be documented and explained so that its rationale is fully understandable to a lawyer. This is all the more important when so much is at stake and the expert's opinion might carry considerable weight in the decision-making process.

Another policy advocated by Aber and Repucci is that experts should indicate *proactively* the limitations of their own information "including presenting conflicting points of view when they are known to the expert" (2, p. 181). Again, we have no objection to these suggestions, because they in no way interfere with the professionals' freedom to do a proper job of assessing and testifying on the matter at hand.

A careful review of the criticism of mental health expertise reveals little that is not correctable. The problems of diagnosis and prediction are inherent in the nature of the complex human problems that psychiatrists and psychologists must deal with. Differences of opinion among professionals arise naturally from such difficulties. In the main, well-trained people afforded ample opportunity to do competent jobs can turn out useful reports. That is the basic premise of this handbook. It is also what the court expects.

In the final analysis, it is for the legal system to decide how and when to call on the expertise of the mental health professional. The latter then must make every effort to provide the service requested in the most scientific, responsible, and sensitive manner. Effective cooperation between the two systems provides the greatest assurance that the best interests of the child will ultimately be served.

REFERENCES

1. Whitebread CH, Heilman J: An overview of the law of juvenile delinquency. Behavioral Sciences and the Law 6(3):285–305, 1988
2. Aber MS, Repucci ND: The limits of mental health expertise in juvenile and family law. Int J Law Psychiatry 10:167–184, 1987

SAMPLE RECOMMENDATIONS

PSYCHIATRIC RECOMMENDATION FOR HOSPITALIZATION

A psychiatric consultant was asked to see Kenny, a 14-year-old boy who was in the juvenile detention building following charges of a serious assault on his mother. He had signed a statement admitting responsibility, and his lawyer had requested an evaluation. The lawyer was concerned about his psychiatric condition. The night of the incident Kenny had been brought home by the police after being arrested for attempting to steal a motor vehicle. After the authorities left, his mother began arguing with Kenny. She was angry because he had been arrested. He became enraged, picked up a hammer, and repeatedly smashed her head, face, and neck, screaming, "I hate you." After she collapsed, Kenny went to a neighbor's apartment. An ambulance was called and the mother was taken to the hospital, where she remained for 2 weeks. She required extensive surgery and the long scar from her head to her neck was quite noticeable during her interview.

Kenny appeared for his interview and evaluation with blandness, lack of affect, and detachment from his account of the incident. He explained a variety of conflicted feelings about his behavior, of "being sorry, feeling all right, and feeling numb about the assault." He suffers nightmares in which he repeats the violence with his mother. He discussed other violent feelings toward "his enemies at school," peers who may tease or fight with him. He has no close friends, and his relationships are shallow. He was not able to talk about any aspect of the relationship with his mother. Further work revealed underlying paranoid ideation, significant disorganization in his thinking, and a major depressive condition.

Considering the serious and violent nature of Kenny's behavior, a recommendation for hospitalization was made to the court before recommendations for disposition could be considered. Further evaluation was deemed to be essential, for both Kenny and his mother, in order to understand what had happened in the past in his family relationships that prompted such a violent reaction.

PSYCHIATRIC RECOMMENDATION FOR CORRECTIONAL SCHOOL

Donald is a 13-year-old charged with assault in the first degree, criminal attempt at murder, and carrying a dangerous weapon. He was adjudicated on the assault charge and while awaiting disposition was again referred to the court on charges identical to the earlier ones but with one additional delinquency: possession of drugs. At the time of psychiatric consultation, neither of Donald's parents appeared for the interview, even though they had been invited.

Donald talked about his involvement in the drug scene and his anger in the dispute over a drug deal that led to the first shooting. He could acknowledge some remorse and fear and stated that he had left detention the first time with a resolve to keep his nose clean. Despite his good intentions, he got back in with the wrong people and again had trouble controlling his anger. His mother's admonitions and his father's attempts to help him did not influence him sufficiently to stay out of trouble. He still thinks about the possibility of a more conventional life, such as working for the telephone company and living on his own, but he tends to be concerned with the day-to-day issues and about what is happening in relation to the court proceedings. He expects to be sent to the correctional school, and he agrees with his mother and his lawyer that it would be best for him to be away for awhile. He thinks he will be able to control his anger while at an institution because he has been able to handle detention without much difficulty.

In summary, Donald appears to be a youngster who is impulsive, angry, and guarded. He tends to be carried away by the feeling of the moment and has little regard for the long-term consequences of his behavior. He does not suffer from a clinical depression or any major psychiatric disorder. He is not ready to return to the community, and he will need long-term educational and rehabilitative efforts to gain control over his impulses so that he can function appropriately in a community.

PSYCHIATRIC EVALUATION FOR A RESIDENTIAL PROGRAM

A psychiatric evaluation for Elizabeth was requested after she was charged with numerous delinquencies, including breach of peace and assault in April, followed by several charges of larceny and assault in November. Elizabeth is a 15-year-old biracial girl who resides currently with her mother and her mother's live-in boyfriend, Arthur. There are no other children in the family. Psychological testing performed just before this evaluation revealed Elizabeth to be of average intelligence. Her scores, however, were felt to underestimate her ability. There was no evidence of impaired reality testing, but the projective tests showed a lack of affective responses and a poor concept of interpersonal relationships.

Both the mother and Arthur are heavy drinkers. He also uses drugs. There is constant fighting within the home, and Arthur is physically abusive toward both Elizabeth and her mother. Although the mother has attempted to end the relationship with him, his threats cause her to be fearful about taking strong action.

The mother said she spoiled Elizabeth during her early life and let her do what she wanted to do. She is aware that Elizabeth is sexually active and does not use contraception. Rather than being concerned about her daughter becoming pregnant, the mother said she would not mind having a baby in the house.

Elizabeth related her delinquencies over the past year to her growing up and wanting to find out what the world is like. What she has learned has been negative, mostly about drugs, violence, and people having problems. She did not mention any positive aspects of her experiences. Last fall the situation at home deteriorated to the point where she left and stayed with a neighbor for 6 weeks. She also did not attend school. Elizabeth denied using drugs and only uses alcohol on "special occasions." She feels she needs to talk, "because if I kept all my feelings inside, I would go crazy." Elizabeth stated that she has never been able to confide in her mother, and as she said this, she fell silent and appeared more depressed. Elizabeth spoke of a sleep disturbance with wakening in the middle of the night and occasional nightmares. Her self-esteem appeared low, and she was unable to make positive statements about herself. During the cognitive portion of the mental status examination she was anxious and self-conscious, as if anticipating failure. Her anxiety appeared to interfere with her ability to concentrate. Her memory was intact, and she was able to think abstractly.

In summary, Elizabeth is a depressed adolescent who is pseudomature and still has many unfulfilled dependency needs. Her mother is helpless and unable to provide emotional support or assist her appropriately in her growth and development. Moreover, she fails to protect her daughter from being the object of physical violence. If the situation continues for Elizabeth, it can only promote further emotional instability, aggressive acting out, and continued delinquencies. Based upon this evaluation, it is recommended that Elizabeth be placed outside the home in a group setting as soon as possible.

EXAMPLES OF TESTIMONY

DIRECT EXAMINATION OF PSYCHIATRIST

By Attorney

Q—Doctor Jones, are you acquainted with one Mary Smith?

A—Yes, I am.

Q—Do you see Miss Smith in the courtroom at this time?

A—Yes, I do.

Q—Would you point her out, please?

A—Yes, right there (indicating).

Q—Have you ever seen Miss Smith before today?

A—Yes, I have.

Q—And when was that?

A—On September 25th, 1989. I attempted to examine her on the unit at Mercywood, but she refused to speak to me.

Q—And for how long a period of time did you . . .

A—I observed her for a period of approximately 30 seconds, I would say.

Q—Other than that 30-second period of observation, and your observations in court today, have you ever seen Miss Smith?

A—No, I haven't.

Q—Have you had occasion to familiarize yourself with the case of Mary Smith?

A—Yes, I have.

Q—And how have you gone about familiarizing yourself with that case?

A—First I interviewed Miss Smith's mother, Mrs. Smith, by telephone for approximately 2 hours on September 21—25th, excuse me. And then, when I arrived at Mercywood, I examined her records, her chart records from this current hospitalization, which began on September

6, 1989, up until the present. I also examined her records from two previous hospitalizations.

And I was able to interview three of the staff who have been caring for Miss Smith. And they included four staff nurses, who see her at least 5 to 6 days a week. A social worker who is her primary counselor. And also the unit psychiatrist.

Q—And is this the information that you relied upon in arriving at your conclusion today?

A—Yes, it is.

Q—And is this the type of information that psychiatrists generally and ordinarily rely upon in arriving at psychiatric conclusions?

A—Yes.

Q—Based on your familiarization of yourself with the case of Mary Smith as you just described to the court, have you an opinion based on a reasonable degree of medical certainty as to whether or not Mary Smith suffers from a mental illness?

A—Yes, I do.

Q—Would you—what is that opinion?

A—That opinion is that she does suffer from a mental illness.

Q—Would you explain to the court the mental illness that in your opinion Mary Smith suffers from?

A—She suffers from what the DSM-III-R, which is the *Diagnostic and Statistical Manual of Psychiatric Disorders* prepared by the American Psychiatric Association, would describe as a psychotic disorder, not otherwise specified.

Q—Could you explain that to the court, please?

A—This is a category of major mental illness or psychosis, which is composed of certain factors from several different types of psychiatric illness, which may involve psychotic disorders and mood disorders, but which does not fit any of the other specific categories of illness because it has some of the characteristics of many.

Q—Would you describe to the court the psychiatric disturbance from which Mary Smith suffers?

A—Yes. Miss Smith suffers from a disorder both of her mood, of her thought process, and also of her behavior.

The disorder of mood involves vacillations between periods of depression, with very low mood, increased appetite, hypersomnia, which is an increased desire for sleep, low self-esteem, a decrease in energy, decrease in concentration and attention. And in addition to that, some feelings that her life may not be worthwhile, may not be worth living any further.

She—interspersed with those periods are sometimes periods of very irritable or euphoric mood in which she has increased energy. She may show considerable impairments in good judgment. She may speak in very loud, rapid fashion. Her conversations may be disjointed and difficult to follow.

In addition to the disorder of mood, she also showed a disorder of her thought process, which is characterized by her speech pattern. And this thought disorder consists, among other things, of delusional beliefs.

At some point in the past she has had what we call grandiose delusions wherein, for example, she has beliefs that she could read other people's minds.

What has been more characteristic of Miss Smith and what she is, in fact, suffering from currently is paranoid delusions. She believes, for example, that people are conspiring against her. At times she has believed that people are following her, wishing to do her harm.

She has also had an ongoing delusion that she is pregnant, despite the fact that she has had several negative pregnancy tests over the last several months, and, in fact, she is menstruating currently.

The thought disorder is also evidenced by the fact that her speech at times becomes disjointed and difficult to follow.

In addition to that, she shows impairments of her judgment, impairments of her concentration. And her attention. Impairments of her insight. And she also shows a certain disturbance in her behavior. That has been manifested in many different ways over the last several months.

Q—With respect to the matter of impairment of judgment, could you explain to the court on what you base that conclusion?

A—Well, information from the sources that I referred to earlier indicated to me that, for example, Miss Smith had prior to this hospitalization in the middle of June gotten into an altercation with another woman over a parking space which culminated in Miss Smith scratching and attempting to choke this woman.

Another example of her impairment of judgment would be more recently. It has been observed while she has been at Elgin that she is very sexually provocative in a way that she uses very poor judgment.

On one occasion she was observed rubbing her breasts up against a male patient, and she was observed by the nursing staff on another occasion to be in the day room sitting in a chair with a short skirt on, with her ankles up on a table, and her knees apart, exposing her vaginal area to several men who were standing behind a glass partition, male patients.

Q—Were there any other examples of impairment of judgment that you recall at the moment?

A—Yes. She has on three or four occasions in the last several months left—before her hospitalization, she has left food burning on a stove unattended, even though she was actually apparently in the apartment or in the house at the time. And this led to a lot of smoke. And on one occasion an actual fire in which the fire department had to be called.

She—there was an episode on August the 18th of 1989, wherein Miss Smith when she was alone in the apartment in Oak Park had an episode in which she threw large cans and other heavy objects against the windows in the apartment, breaking seven of the eight windows in the apartment, and—causing shattered glass to fly throughout the apartment and also some of it onto the sidewalk below.

Q—With respect to the matter of impairment of concentration, could you describe to the court what—to what you're referring?

A—Yes. The impairment of concentration is a symptom that I deduce from the fact that she has been observed on occasion to be sitting 10 or 15 feet away from food which is burning on the stove, which she had started, and watching television, and being apparently unaware of the fact that there was a fire starting.

In addition to that, there were—there have been two documented automobile accidents that occurred, one, I believe, in June, and one in July. One in which Miss Smith backed into another automobile. Another in which she rear-ended an automobile. And these incidents led to her having her automobile insurance revoked, as a matter of fact.

I deduce from that that there was some impairment in her concentration and attention.

Q—With respect to the matter of impairment of insight, could you describe to the court the basis for that conclusion?

A—Yes. The fact that Miss Smith adamantly and strongly refuses to acknowledge the fact that she suffers from a mental illness, and that she needs treatment, particularly that she needs medication, I think, shows an impairment in her insight to the point where it will make recovery or even improvement from this illness outside of a secure hospital facility, in particular, very difficult, if not impossible.

Q—Calling your attention to the matter of Miss Smith's psychiatric history, if any, and history with respect to medication, if any, are you aware at all, Doctor, and if so, would you describe to the court any aspect of that history that in any way contributes to your conclusions with respect to these impairments?

A—Yes. My understanding is that Miss Smith was treated with a combination of lithium, which is a mood-stabilizing agent used primarily for bipolar disorders, and Navane, which is an antipsychotic agent, used to treat disturbances of behavior and thought process.

She was on those medications from approximately August of 1987 to roughly January or February, I believe, of 1989. And during that period of time, her illness was under fairly good control, and she, in fact, functioned quite nicely. She went to school. Her mother describes good self-confidence, normal appetite, normal sleep. She did very well.

Q—What, if any, information have you subsequent to that time that supports your conclusions with respect to those issues?

A—My understanding is that Miss Smith began to deteriorate very rapidly in her functioning, as I've described, shortly after stopping her medications early in the—in the early part of 1989.

Q—What, if any, information have you as to Miss Smith's position with respect to taking medication at this time?

A—I have information from all of the sources which I referred to earlier that she very strongly is opposed to taking any form of medication for her mental illness at this time or in the future.

Q—What, if anything, does that indicate to you with respect to the matter of insight?

A—It indicates to me that she has an impairment in her insight and judgment in that she has probably, because of the mental illness, she has an inability to recognize the fact that she is sick, and that she has this disturbance in her behavior, her mood, her thought process, her judgment, and because of that, she is either unwilling or unable to accept recommended standard treatment that will help her to overcome the illness.

Q—Calling your attention, Doctor, to the third category you mentioned, the category of disturbances of behavior, could you please describe to the court what it is you mean with respect to that?

A—Well, some of them I have referred to earlier. The episodes wherein fires were started and when food was left cooking unattended, probably inadvertently on her part, while she was still in the house or in the apartment.

The episode of August 18th where the damage was caused in the apartment, windows were broken, there was flying glass, some of which landed inside, some of which landed outside the apartment on the sidewalk below.

The automobile accidents that I referred to earlier.

The incident with the woman over the parking space that led to the battery charge against Miss Smith in the middle of July of '89.

In addition to that, and more recently while she has been in the hospital, she has shown peculiarities in her behavior that have manifested themselves as unwillingness or inability to take care of her personal hygiene appropriately. She has been unable or unwilling to bathe. To change her clothes properly.

And, in fact, my understanding is that last week she was having her menstrual period and she did not wear any sanitary protection to the point where other patients were complaining about the mess and the odor, and it took several staff persons together to convince her, to somehow elicit her cooperation to bathe and to properly take care of her hygiene in that regard.

Q—Doctor—

A—Excuse me. There's also the sexual provocativeness that I referred to earlier and acting that out on the hospital ward.

Q—Doctor, are there any other matters that you feel should be brought to the attention of the court with respect to your conclusion that Miss Smith suffers from a mental illness, or have I covered them all?

A—I—I would say that there is one more matter, and that is that the—although there has not been the same degree of dangerous behavior, such as the breaking of windows and setting fires while she has been in the hospital, that is because in a hospital setting, a person is very carefully monitored, very carefully watched, it's a very enclosed, secure, monitored facility.

And what is important is that there is no indication that Miss Smith off of her medication, even though she's in the hospital, has had an improvement in her basic underlying mental illness. And therefore, were she out of the hospital, she would most likely very quickly regress to the same forms of dangerous behavior that she did before.

Q—Doctor, have you an opinion based on a reasonable degree of medical certainty as to whether or not Mary Smith is reasonably expected in the near future to inflict serious physical harm upon herself or another?

A—Yes, I do.

Q—And what is your opinion?

A—My opinion is that she is reasonably expected, if she is outside of a secure hospital setting, to inflict serious harm upon herself or another in the near future.

Q—Could you explain to the court, please, on what you base that conclusion?

A—I base that conclusion on the information that I derived from the various sources that I referred to earlier, hospital chart, interviews with staff, and interview with family.

Q—And specifically, of those matters which you described to the court, what leads you to conclude that there's a reasonable expectation of imminent harm?

A—It is primarily the behavioral disturbances that I referred to. Such as the inadvertent fire setting. The smashing of glass. The automobile accidents which are probably from impaired concentration and attention. The aggressive action which led to the battery charge being filed against her. The sexual provocativeness and the impaired judgment which she showed which could lead to disastrous consequences for her. And, also, the inability to care for her basic hygiene.

Q—Doctor, have you an opinion based on a reasonable degree of medical certainty as to whether or not Mary Smith can care for herself so as to provide for her basic needs and to guard herself from harm?

A—Yes, I do.

Q—And what is your opinion?

A—My opinion is that again outside of a secure hospital setting, she would be unable to provide for her basic needs so as to guard herself from harm.

Q—Could you explain to the court why it is you feel that that's the case?

A—I feel that way because of the behavioral disturbances and also the lack of insight which she reveals. The fire setting. The smashing of glass. The sexual provocativeness and the impaired judgment which could lead to very serious consequences.

And in addition to that, the impairment of judgment that seems to prevent her from recognizing that she is ill and needs treatment, such that recovery will be extremely difficult for this young woman, short of hospitalization and required treatment.

Q—Doctor, is there any other aspect that I've neglected to ask you about which you feel would assist the court in its determination with respect to the matter of reasonable expectation of harm or inability to care for herself that you would like the court to know about?

A—Yes. I think there is one other factor, and that is that there has been a very obvious gradual deterioration in her overall functioning as an independent adult since early in 1989 when she stopped her medication. And that has been manifested in several different ways.

She was expelled from school. Her family is at risk for eviction from their apartment because of the incident I referred to earlier with the breaking of windows. She has lost her automobile insurance. She has been sexually provocative and inappropriate. And all of the other matters that I referred to earlier show a gradual deterioration in her functioning, which I believe would make it very difficult, if not impossible, for her to live in a safe way outside of the hospital right now.

Q—Doctor, specifically, would you describe for the court what in your opinion is the least restrictive environment in which Miss Smith could be treated at the present time?

A—Yes. Given the state of illness currently, and the fact that she is refusing medications, I believe that the least restrictive environment in which she could be safely treated right now is a secure hospital setting.

Q—And have you an opinion, Doctor, based on a reasonable degree of medical certainty, as to whether that situation would change if Miss Smith would be willing to take medication?

A—That situation would be likely to change and to improve drastically if she were to take medications. It's difficult for me to predict exactly how long that may take because it varies tremendously from patient to patient.

Based on my information about her response during the previous hospitalization, it would probably take somewhere in the vicinity of 4 to 6 weeks.

Q—No further questions.

Example of Line of Questions to Be Asked to Qualify a Mental Health Professional as an Expert Witness

- Please state your full name for the record.
- What is your profession?
- Where do you practice? Would you please describe the nature of your practice to the court?
- Are you licensed to practice medicine in the state of Illinois?
- Since when? Do you hold any other licenses?
- Would you please describe to the court the education you received to become a psychiatrist. Did you graduate?
- What degree did you receive? Do you hold any other graduate degrees?
- Have you participated in a residency training program?
- Where did you receive that training?
- In your postgraduate psychiatry training, did you concentrate in a specific area of psychiatry?
- As part of your psychiatric training, have you taken courses in child and adolescent development?
- Have you been the recipient of any awards, honors, or prizes?
- Are you board eligible/certified?
- When did you become board certified?
- Do you belong to any professional associations? Would you please name some of them for the court? Do you now or have you in the past held any offices or committee appointments? Please describe.
- Since completing your psychiatric training, have you engaged in any continuing professional education? Please describe this to the court.
- Are you affiliated with a hospital?
- With what hospitals have you been affiliated in the past?
- Do you hold any academic post?
- Have you engaged in any research? Please describe it.
- Have you written any articles? Please tell the court about several of them.
- How many children/adolescents/families [whatever is relevant to the case] would you say that you have evaluated/treated during your career as a psychiatrist?
- What type of work did you do with them?
- How often do you normally see children/adolescents/families who are in treatment with you?

- In general, how long are your sessions?
- Have you had cases dealing with parenting/child abuse/sexual deviancy issues? How many?
- Dr. Jones, I show you a document entitled "Curriculum Vitae," bearing your name and marked Respondent's Exhibit 7 for identification. Is this your resume? Does it truly and accurately reflect your professional experience and training? (Attorney will show a copy to opposing counsel and offer it into evidence.)
- Your Honor, at this time, I offer Dr. Jones as an expert witness in psychiatry and in the field of parenting and child development [child abuse/sexual deviancy . . .]. May I proceed?
- Are you acquainted with Joe Doakes?
- How did you become acquainted with him? How many times have you seen him? When? What was the nature of your evaluation? Did you take a history? etc.
- How long were your interviews with Joe? His parents? etc.
- Did you cause any psychological tests to be performed? Describe.
- Did you have occasion to review any records? Describe.
- Is this the kind of information that psychiatrists generally rely upon in forming their clinical conclusions and opinion?
- Based upon your evaluation of Joe (the family . . . etc.), have you an opinion based upon a degree of psychiatric certainty as to whether Joe suffers from a psychiatric or other disturbance?
- (And/or other questions to be answered for the court.)
- What is that opinion? On what do you base that opinion?

It is most important that the expert witness go over his or her resume and background with the presenting attorney prior to the hearing. Any problems or weaknesses should be pointed out and discussed with the attorney so that he or she can properly frame the questioning to minimize them and maximize the positives. Occasionally, attorneys will go so far as to carefully check out the facts presented. Obviously, the resume should be entirely accurate. The attorney will omit questions about authorship, prizes, etc., where these are not part of your experience.

APPENDIX   3

CONSENT FOR EVALUATION

_____ , a minor,

and _____ , his or her parent

or guardian, consent to the psychiatric/psychological/psychosocial evaluation of

_____ by

_____ as follows:

_____	_____
Name of person being evaluated	Date of birth
_____	_____
Address	Social security number
_____	_____
Address	Telephone number

We understand that the evaluation is being done for purposes of a case presently

pending in Juvenile Court under case no _____.

The evaluation has been

_____ ordered by the Court.

_____ requested by the defense counsel.

_____ other: _____

_____

The evaluation will consist of the following:

_____ interviews by Dr. _____

with _____

_____

_____

_____

_____ psychological testing

_____ physical examination

_____ laboratory tests (specify)

_____

_____

_____

_____ other procedures

_____

_____

_____

The purpose of the evaluation is to provide the following information:

The information gathered during the evaluation will be disclosed to the following persons:

The information might be used or disclosed as follows:

The risks to me (my child) if I cooperate and disclose confidential information during the evaluation are:

The risks if I do not cooperate and disclose confidential information during the evaluation are:

I do/do not consent to audio/video taping of interviews.

I understand that my attorney has a right to inspect and copy notes and records of the evaluator.

Minor	Date

Parent/Guardian	Date

Witness	Date

Witness	Date

N.B. In some jurisdictions, a patient or his or her parent or guardian has a right to see, inspect, and copy any mental health record, including evaluation reports. Check this out with the lawyer or court officer who has requested your services.

SAMPLE REFERRAL FORM

COURT OF COMMON PLEAS
JUVENILE COURT DIVISION

Referral for Clinical Evaluation

Please complete this form and bring it to the clinic. The court record or a copy of the most recent predispositional report must accompany this referral for an appointment to be made.

Thank you for your cooperation.

Name _____ Record no _____

Date of birth _____ Telephone no _____

Address with zip code _____

_____

Court date _____ Date of referral _____

Jurist _____ P.O./D.H.S. _____ Supervisor _____

School and grade _____

Legal complaint _____ Rule #30 _____ Yes ____ No ____

Current placement _____ Home _____ DC _____ C _____ HD

Reason for Referral (check any that apply)

( )   Aggression: ____ Assault

____Use of weapon; specify: _____

____Lock up in DC

( )   Anxiety: _____ Pacing _____ Shaky

( )   Bizarre behavior; describe: _____

( )   Confusion

( )   Depression

( )   Eating problems

( )   Family assessment: _____Custody pending

_____Parental termination motion pending

_____Abuse/neglect action pending

_____Influence of family on youth's functioning

( )   Fire setting

( )   Learning problem

( )   Management problem in DC

( )   Medical condition's influence on behavior

( )   Medication review

( )   Mental health services review

( )   Overactivity

( )   Placement planning

( )   Sexual history

( )   Sleeping problems

( )   Substance abuse

( )   Suicide history; describe: _____

_____

( )   Withdrawn behavior

( )   Other; describe: _____

_____

_____

For office use only
Clinician(s) _____
_____

LIST OF LANDMARK DECISIONS

Application of Paul L. GAULT.
387 U.S. 1, 1,7 S.CT. 1428 (1967)

In this case, a 15-year-old boy was committed as a juvenile delinquent to a state industrial school. The boy's parents, attempting to have him released, here appeal from a dismissal of a petition from a writ of habeas corpus by the Arizona Supreme Court, 99 Ariz. 181, 407 P.2d 760. "The United States Supreme Court, Mr. Justice Fortas, held that juvenile has right to notice of charges, to counsel, to confrontation and cross-examination of witnesses, and to privilege against self-incrimination."

Morris A. KENT, Jr., Petitioner,
v.
UNITED STATES.
383 U.S. 541, 86 S.CT. 1045 (1966)

Here, a juvenile was arrested and prosecuted for housebreaking and robbery. The United States District Court for the District of Columbia entered judgments of conviction on the counts of housebreaking and robbery and the defendant appealed. The United States Court of Appeals for the District of Columbia, 119 U.S.App.D.C. 378, 343 F.2d 247, affirmed and certiorari was granted. The Supreme Court, Mr. Justice Fortas, held that under District of Columbia Juvenile Court Act the Juvenile Court may waive jurisdiction over a juvenile after full investigation. Furthermore, the court held that in order to have a valid waiver order the juvenile must be entitled to a hearing, including access by his counsel to the social records and probation or similar reports which were considered by court, and to a statement of reasons for the Juvenile Court's decision.

In the Matter of Samuel WINSHIP, Appellant.
397 U.S. 358, 90 S.CT. 1068 (1970)

In a juvenile delinquency proceeding the Family Court, Bronx County, adjudged Samuel Winship to be a juvenile delinquent, and he appealed.

The Supreme Court, Appellate Division, affirmed, 30 A.D.2d 781, 291 N.Y.S.2d 1005. Samuel Winship then appealed to the Court of Appeals on constitutional grounds, and the order was again affirmed, 24 N.Y.2d 196, 299 N.Y.S.2d 414, 247 N.E.2d 253. The Supreme Court, Mr. Justice Brennan, reversed and held that the reasonable-doubt standard of criminal law has constitutional stature and that juveniles, like adults, are constitutionally entitled to proof beyond reasonable doubt when they are charged with a violation of a criminal law.

HALEY
v.
STATE OF OHIO.
332 U.S. 596, 68 S.CT. 302 (1948)

A 15-year-old boy confessed to murder after five hours of interrogation by police officers and without the police officers' warning the boy of his right to the benefit of the advice of friends, family, or counsel. The boy, John Harvey Haley, was convicted of murder in the first degree. Judgment of conviction was affirmed by the Court of Appeals of Ohio, 79 Ohio App. 237, 72 N.E.2d 785. Appeal from the Court of Appeals was dismissed by the Supreme Court of Ohio, 147 Ohio St. 340, 70 N.E.2d 905, and defendant brings certiorari. The Supreme Court held that the confession should have been excluded because of the involuntary method used to extract the confession and that the method was violative of the due process requirements of Fourteenth Amendment. U.S.C.A.Const. Amend 14.

Joseph MCKEIVER and Edward Terry, Appellants,
v.
State of PENNSYLVANIA.
In re Barbara BURRUS et al., Petitioners.
403 U.S. 528, 91 S.CT. 1976 (1971)

Juveniles were adjudged delinquents and on appeal the Superior Court, 215 Pa.Super. 760, 255 A.2d 921 and 215 Pa.Super. 762, 255 A.2d 922, the order was affirmed, and leave to appeal was granted. The Supreme Court of Pennsylvania, 438 Pa. 339, 265 A.2d 350, affirmed and the Supreme Court noted probable jurisdiction. In another related case, juveniles were declared delinquents and on appeal the North Carolina Court of Appeals, 4 N.C.App. 523, 167 S.E.2d 454, affirmed. On appeal the Supreme Court of North Carolina, 275 N.C. 517, 169 S.E.2d 879, modified and affirmed, and certiorari was granted.

The Supreme Court, Mr. Justice Blackmun, announced the court's judgments and delivered an opinion determining that trial by jury in adjudicative stage of state juvenile court delinquency proceeding is not constitutionally required.

Peter STANLEY, Sr., Petitioner,
v.
State of ILLINOIS.
405 U.S. 645, 92 S.CT. 1208 (1972)

Dependency proceeding was brought by State of Illinois upon the death of the natural mother of the children. The determination of the Circuit Court of Cook County, John P. McGury, J., that the children were dependent was affirmed by the Supreme Court of Illinois, 45 Ill.2d 132, 256 N.E.2d 814. The children's natural father brought certiorari. The Supreme Court, Mr. Justice White, held that under the Due Process Clause of the Fourteenth Amendment, unwed father was entitled to hearing on his fitness as parent before his children could be taken from him in dependency proceeding instituted by the State of Illinois after the death of the children's natural mother.

John F. TINKER and Mary Beth Tinker,
Minors, etc., et al., Petitioners,
v.
DES MOINES INDEPENDENT COMMUNITY
SCHOOL DISTRICT et al.
393 U.S. 503, 89 S.CT. 733 (1969)

Action against school district, its board of directors and certain administrative officials and teachers to recover nominal damages and obtain an injunction against enforcement of a regulation promulgated by principals of schools prohibiting wearing of black armbands by students while on school facilities. The United States District Court for the Southern District of Iowa, Central Division, 258 F.Supp. 971, dismissed complaint and plaintiffs appealed. The Court of Appeals for the Eighth Circuit, 383 F.2d 988, considered the case en banc and affirmed without opinion and certiorari was granted.

The United States Supreme Court, Mr. Justice Fortas, held that, "in absence of demonstration of any facts which might reasonably have led school authorities to forecast substantial disruption of, or material interference with, school activities or any showing that disturbances or disorders on school premises in fact occurred when students wore black armbands on their sleeves to exhibit their disapproval of Vietnam hostilities, regulation prohibiting wearing armbands to schools and providing for suspension of any student refusing to remove such was an unconstitutional denial of students' right of expression of opinion."

James PARHAM, Individually and as Commissioner of the Department of Human Resources, et al., Appellants,
v.
J.R. et al.
442 U.S. 584, 584, 99 S.CT. 2493 (S.CT., 1979)

Minor children brought action alleging that they and other class members had been deprived of their liberty without procedural due process by virtue of Georgia mental health laws which permit voluntary admission of minor children to mental hospitals by parents or guardians. The Court for the United States District Court for the Middle District of Georgia, 412 F.Supp. 112, ruled the laws unconstitutional. On appeal, the Supreme Court, Mr. Chief Justice Burger, ruled that Georgia's procedures for admitting a child for treatment to a state mental hospital are reasonable and consistent with constitutional guarantees. The court further held that the risk of error inherent in parental decision to have a child institutionalized for mental health care is sufficiently great that some kind of inquiry should be made by a "neutral fact finder" to determine whether statutory requirements for admission are satisfied. Such a "fact finding" need not be conducted by an individual that is law-trained nor is it required that the fact finding be made by a judicial or administrative officer. Such an inquiry must look into the child's background using all available sources and it is necessary that decision maker have authority to refuse to admit child who does not satisfy medical standards for admission. The continuing need for commitment should be reviewed periodically by a similarly independent procedure.

Milton R. DUSKY, Petitioner,
v.
UNITED STATES of America.
362 U.S. 402, 80 S.CT. 788 (1960)

Defendant was convicted of unlawfully transporting in interstate commerce a girl who had been kidnapped. The United States Court of Appeals, Eighth Circuit, 271 F.2d 385, affirmed, and defendant petitioned for certiorari. The Supreme Court, Per Curiam, held that record insufficiently supported finding of competency to stand trial. The court noted that the "test of a defendant's competency to stand trial is whether he has sufficient present ability to consult with his lawyer with a reasonable degree of rational understanding and whether he has rational as well as factual understanding of proceeding against him; it is not enough that he is oriented to time and place and has some recollection of events." 18 U.S.C.A. s 4244.

John SANTOSKY II and Annie SANTOSKY, Petitioners
v.
Bernhardt S. KRAMER, Commissioner, Ulster County Department of Social Services, et al.
455 U.S. 745, 102 S.CT. 1388 (1982)

Parents appealed from judgment of the Family Court, Ulster County, Elwyn, J., which adjudged their children to be permanently neglected. The New York Supreme Court, Appellate Division, affirmed, 75 A.D.2d 910, 427 N.Y.S.2d 319. The New York Court of Appeals dismissed the parents' appeal. Certiorari was granted. The Supreme Court, Mr. Justice Blackmun, held that "before a state may sever completely and irrevocably the rights of parents in their natural child, due process requires that the state support its allegations by at least clear and convincing evidence that the parents are not competent to care for their children." Therefore, the "fair preponderance of the evidence" standard prescribed by the New York Family Court Act for the termination of parental rights denies the parents due process.

Ellen SCHALL, Commissioner of New York City Department of Juvenile Justice
v.
Gregory MARTIN et al.
Robert ABRAMS, Attorney General of New York
v.
Gregory MARTIN et al.
467 U.S. 253, 104 S.CT. 2403 (1984)

Juveniles who had been detained under a section of New York Family Court Act authorizing pretrial detention brought habeas corpus action seeking declaratory judgment that the statute in question violated, inter alia, the due process clause. The United States District Court for the Southern District of New York, 513 F.Supp. 691, struck down the statute. On appeal, the United States Court of Appeals for the Second Circuit, 689 F.2d 365, affirmed, and probable jurisdiction was noted, 103 S.Ct. 1765. The Supreme Court, Justice Rehnquist, held that section of New York Family

Court Act authorizing pretrial detention of accused juvenile delinquent based on finding that there was "serious risk" that juvenile "may before the return date commit an act which if committed by an adult would constitute a crime" did not violate due process clause.

William Wayne THOMPSON, Petitioner
v.
OKLAHOMA.
487 U.S. 815, 108 S.CT. 2687 (1988)

Defendant was convicted of first-degree murder and sentenced to death, by jury verdict, in the District Court of Grady County, James R. Winchester, J. Defendant appealed. The Oklahoma Court of Criminal Appeals, 724 P.2d 780, Brett, J., affirmed. On writ of certiorari, the Supreme Court, Justice Stevens, held that Eighth and Fourteenth Amendments prohibited execution of defendant convicted of first-degree murder for offense committed when defendant was 15 years old.

Kevin N. STANFORD, Petitioner
v.
KENTUCKY.
Heath A. WILKINS, Petitioner
v.
MISSOURI.
109 S.CT. 2969 (1989)

A defendant who was approximately 17 years and 4 months old at the time he committed a murder in Kentucky was convicted of murder, sodomy, robbery, and receiving stolen property and was sentenced to death by the Jefferson Circuit Court, Charles M. Leibson, J. Defendant appealed. The Supreme Court of Kentucky, 734 S.W.2d 781, affirmed. In another case, a defendant who was approximately 16 years and 6 months old when he committed a murder in Missouri was certified for trial as an adult. He was convicted in the Circuit Court, Clay County, Glennon E. McFarland, J., of first-degree murder and sentenced to death, and he appealed. The Supreme Court of Missouri, 736 S.W.2d 409, Billings, C.J., affirmed. On certiorari, the Supreme Court, Justice Scalia, held that imposition of capital punishment on an individual for a crime committed at 16 or 17 years of age did not violate evolving standards of decency and thus did not constitute cruel and unusual punishment under the Eighth Amendment.

SAMPLE CONTRACT WITH THE COURT

EMPLOYMENT [OR CONSULTATION] CONTRACT

This Agreement, made this _____ day of November, 1990, (hereinafter the effective date), between THE JUVENILE COURT OF HAPPY COUNTY, STATE, (hereinafter THE COURT) and ROBERT C. JONES, M.D. (hereinafter THE CONSULTANT) of 10238 South Kenilworth Avenue, Blisstown, State.

WHEREAS, THE COURT from time to time requires a psychiatric evaluation of clients and families related to matters before it; and

WHEREAS, THE COURT wishes to employ THE CONSULTANT as a psychiatrist to conduct psychiatric evaluations of COURT clients and families for such compensation and other benefits hereinafter set forth; and

WHEREAS, THE CONSULTANT is licensed to practice medicine pursuant to the Medical Practice Act of State and is board eligible/certified in psychiatry; and

WHEREAS, THE CONSULTANT wishes to accept employment from THE COURT on the terms stated herein.

NOW, THEREFORE, in consideration of the premises, the covenants and the following provisions, the parties agree as follows:

1. **EMPLOYMENT.** THE COURT hereby employs THE CONSULTANT, and THE CONSULTANT hereby accepts employment from THE COURT upon the terms and conditions set forth herein.

2. **TERM.** The term of this agreement shall begin on December 3, 1990, and shall continue until December 2, 1991, and for such additional terms as the parties may thereafter agree in writing, subject, however, to termination at any time upon ninety (90) days' written notice by either THE COURT or THE CONSULTANT, each to the other, unless otherwise limited by this Agreement. This Agreement is conditional upon THE CONSULTANT being and remaining (a) a licensed physician in good

standing in the state of _____, (b) duly accredited to practice psychiatry, (c) physically and mentally able to fulfill his/her duties hereunder, (d) free of any adverse finding by any relevant professional association ethics board, and (e) being eligible for malpractice coverage in an amount not less than $1 million–$3 million, failing any of which this Agreement and all rights and obligations thereunder shall be subject, at the option of THE COURT, to immediate termination or renegotiation.

3. **COMPENSATION.** For all services rendered by THE CONSULTANT under this Agreement, THE COURT will pay to THE CONSULTANT a salary of $60,000. per year **[or: the sum of $xxx per hour/procedure, etc. If the consultant is an independent contractor, not an employee, there should be a recital as to tax liability. Any benefits available to the consultant, e.g., vacation, disability pay, insurance, continuing education, etc., should be spelled out here.]**

4. **RESTRICTIONS ON CONSULTANT; CONFLICTS OF INTEREST. [Any restrictions on the consultant's practice outside the court should be set out here, e.g., is (s)he permitted to take other forensic cases, render treatment services to court clients, etc.]**

5. **MALPRACTICE INSURANCE.** It is a condition of this Agreement that THE CONSULTANT maintain at his or her own expense professional liability insurance coverage in the minimum amount of $1 million–$3 million. **[or for a court employee: there should be a recital to the effect that the court will defend and indemnify the consultant against any claim or judgment arising out of the consultant's activities for and on behalf of the court.]**

6. **DUTIES.** THE CONSULTANT will be available to THE COURT for _____ hours each week/month and shall perform duties as follows:

[You may wish to spell out who the consultant's supervisor or court liaison and legal consultant is, specific hours of employment, on-call responsibilities, etc.] THE CONSULTANT is required to keep records as required by the Policies and Procedures Manual of THE COURT and such other records and statistics as are from time to time directed by the Supervisor.

THE CONSULTANT certifies that (s)he is familiar with the State Mental Health and Developmental Code, the Mental Health Confidentiality Act, and the Juvenile Court Act, and that (s)he will perform his/her duties in accordance therewith and in accordance with the standard of care recognized by psychiatrists in the community, the requirements and standards of the State Medical Practice Act and the ethical principles of the American Psychiatric Association and other bodies, formal, informal, governmental or otherwise, to whom psychiatrists look for direction and guidance, and to whom they are subject to licensing and control.

7. **OFFICE FACILITIES AND EQUIPMENT.** THE COURT will furnish to THE CONSULTANT furnished office space, equipment, stationery and supplies, secretarial help, telephone and pager service, and such other facilities and services suitable and adequate for his/her position and the performance of his/her duties. [or, e.g.: **THE CONSULTANT will provide services in his/her offices located at _____. THE CONSULTANT will provide to THE COURT evidence of premises liability insurance as follows: ____]**

8. **EXPENSES.** THE CONSULTANT is required by this contract to own, lease, or otherwise have available an automobile for his/her regular use in performing services hereunder at his/her own expense. (S)he will at all times maintain at his/her own expense automobile liability insurance in the face amount of not less than $500,000. and will provide to THE COURT evidence of such insurance from time to time. Further, the insurance contract shall specifically provide that THE COURT shall be protected against liability arising out of THE CONSULTANT'S use of the automobile in the performance of his/her duties hereunder. Upon presentation of documentation reflecting mileage and tolls required for the performance of his/her duties, THE COURT will reimburse THE CONSULTANT therefor at the rate of .26 per mile. Except as otherwise provided herein, THE CONSULTANT will be personally responsible for his/her expenses connected with the services provided hereunder. THE COURT, at its sole discretion, may from time to time reimburse THE CONSULTANT for certain of those expenses; however, THE CONSULTANT's obligations with respect to these matters are unconditional and not dependent upon reimbursement. [**Consult a tax advisor re specific terms for this paragraph which will permit maximum income tax deductions, especially if you are an employee and not an independent contractor.]**

9. **GOVERNING LAW.** This Agreement shall be subject to and governed by the laws of the state of _____, irrespective of the fact that THE CONSULTANT is or may become a resident of another state. Venue shall be _____ County.

10. **ENTIRE AGREEMENT.** This Document constitutes the entire agreement between the parties and contains all of the agreements between the parties with respect to the subject matter hereof; this Agreement supersedes any and all other agreements, whether oral or in writing, between the parties hereto with respect to the subject matter hereof. No change or modification of this Agreement shall be valid unless the same be in writing

and signed by THE COURT and THE CONSULTANT. No waiver of any provisions of this Agreement shall be valid unless in writing and signed by the person or party to be charged.

11. **SEVERABILITY.** If any portion or portions of this Agreement shall be, for any reason, invalid or unenforceable, the remaining portion or portions shall nevertheless be valid, enforceable, and carried into effect, unless to do so would clearly violate the present legal and valid intention of the parties hereto.

12. **NOTICES.** Any and all notices, designations, consents, offers, acceptances, or other communication provided for herein shall be given in writing by personal delivery or by registered or certified mail, return receipt requested, which shall be addressed to each party at the address set forth hereinabove, or such later address as may from time to time be provided by each in writing. All notices shall be deemed effective upon personal delivery or mailing.

13. **ARBITRATION.** In the event of a dispute between the parties hereto, the parties agree to submit the dispute for resolution to an arbitrator who is a panel member of the American Arbitration Association (AAA). Within one (1) week following notice by any party to this Agreement of the inability to reach agreement, each party shall have the obligation to choose an arbitrator by alternately striking names from a list provided by the AAA; the remaining named person shall forthwith arbitrate the fact or matter in dispute and arrive at a decision within two (2) weeks. If a party does not comply with the terms of this provision and choose such arbitrator as provided herein, then the arbitrator chosen by the party who shall have complied with this provision shall choose the arbitrator. The decision of the arbitrator shall be final and binding to all parties hereto and enforceable by legal action. The cost of the arbitration proceeding shall be borne equally by the parties.

IN WITNESS WHEREOF, the parties have executed this Agreement on the date first and above written.

THE COURT

by _____

ROBERT C. JONES, M.D.

MENTAL STATUS EXAMINATION

The mental status examination is an organized description of the patient. Together with the psychiatric history, the mental status examination makes up the bulk of every psychiatric evaluation. The term refers to the direct observation and questioning of the patient and is composed of a standard series of components. Depending on the nature of the case, greater emphasis may be placed on the assessment of particular components. Thus, for a delinquent adolescent, the issue of *social judgment* may be of particular concern, whereas for a young child alleged to have been sexually abused, the question of *clinical credibility* takes on critical importance.

The major elements of the mental status examination are as follows:

- **Appearance and behavior.** This includes physical characteristics, dress, manner, speech, and attitude. Any unusual observations such as stiff posture or the presence of grimaces or tics should be noted. Hostility to the examiner is a significant finding suggestive of a pattern of antiauthoritarian angry feelings.

- **Emotions.** Spontaneous descriptions of feelings and/or responses to questions about feelings refer to the mood of the patient. In addition, visible signs of what the patient is experiencing emotionally (downcast look, nervousness) should be recorded. This range of affective expression and its intensity are valuable clues to the psychological state of the individual. Affect (visibly expressed emotion) may also be either appropriate or inappropriate to the circumstances or to the subject being discussed.

- **Perception.** The senses may be intact or may reflect severe disturbances in which reality is misperceived or distorted. Hallucinations are false sensory perceptions and may include any of the senses. Hallucinations are found in psychotic illnesses.

- **Thought processes.** Disturbances can involve both the form and the content of thinking. Thinking may be slowed, incoherent, irrelevant, or disorganized. The thought content may include obsessions (persistently repetitive ideas) or, in psychosis, delusions (fixed false ideas).

- **Sensorium and cognition.** *Sensorium* refers to the level of consciousness and the orientation to person, place, and time. *Cognition* refers generally to intellectual functioning, including intelligence, general information, memory, and capacity for abstract thinking. Abnormalities in this area may suggest organic disorders or intellectual deficits.

- **Impulses and drives.** How an individual manages, controls, and directs aggressive and sexual impulses is important to an understanding of behavior disorders. A description of the intensity of the drives and the nature of their expression is helpful to an understanding of the juvenile population.

- **Judgment.** Commonsense judgment and judgment in a variety of social situations are assessed.

- **Insight.** This involves the degree of self-understanding or awareness of what is going on psychologically and how it is related to the individual's behavior and problems.

- **Reliability.** Any interview data relevant to the patient's credibility should be described.

G L O S S A R Y

Abused child Any child who has been subjected to cruelty resulting in physical, moral, or mental damage. Physical abuse may include sexual exploitation of the child.

Adjudicatory hearing or adjudication The court procedure at which the charges are heard and the judge determines whether or not they are true.

Bind over See *waiver*.

Certification The transfer, by a juvenile court, of the case to another county in the state where the juvenile resides. In addition, a court may transfer a custody order to another state through the Interstate Compact. Also used in some jurisdictions to describe transfer to adult court.

Certiorari A higher court asking a lower court for the record of a case for review.

CHINS Child in need of supervision. See *status offender*.

Commitment In juvenile law, describes placement in a mental health facility. A court-ordered act placing children who are declared delinquent, neglected, dependent, or uncared for under the jurisdiction of the state's children and youth agency.

Competency A legal finding; the person charged has a rational and factual grasp of the charges and proceedings and he or she is able to cooperate with the attorney in his or her own defense with a reasonable degree of rational understanding.

Confidentiality A legal and ethical duty of a psychiatrist not to disclose information obtained in the course of rendering professional services, except with the informed consent of the patient or client (or parent or guardian if a minor) except as is otherwise required or permitted by law.

Court advocate See *guardian ad litem*.

Custody The care and control of a thing or person. The keeping, guarding, care, watch, inspection, preservation, or security of a thing, carrying with it the idea of the thing being within the immediate personal care and control of the person to whose custody it is subjected. Immediate charge and control, and not the final, absolute control of ownership, implying responsibility for the protection and preservation of the thing in custody.

Also, the detainer of an individual's person by virtue of lawful process or authority.

The term is very elastic and may mean actual imprisonment, or physical detention, or mere power, legal or physical, of imprisoning, or of taking manual possession. Term "custody" within statute requiring that petitioner be "in custody" to be entitled to federal habeas corpus relief does not necessarily mean actual physical detention in jail or prison, but rather is synonymous with restraint of liberty.

Deinstitutionalization In juvenile justice, not putting status offenders in secure facilities. In psychiatric care, discharge from hospital to community, particularly of those chronically mentally ill patients who would otherwise be kept in hospital for long periods of time.

Delinquent child A youth under the mandated age in the statutes of each state who has committed an act that would be a crime if committed by an adult.

Dependent child A child who is homeless or destitute or without proper care or support through no fault of his or her parent, guardian, or custodian; who lacks proper care or support by reason of the mental or physical condition of his or her parent, guardian, or custodian; or whose condition or environment is such as to warrant that the state, in the interests of the child, assumes guardianship.

Disposition In criminal procedure, the sentencing or other final settlement of a criminal case. In juvenile court, the determination by the juvenile court judge, based on all information available concerning the youth (which may include family history, psychological and psychiatric evaluation, educational information, victim impact statements, etc.), of what is in the best interests of the youth and the safety of the community. The goal is habilitation or rehabilitation of the youth.

Domestic relations That branch or discipline of the law that deals with matters of the household or family, including divorce, separation, custody, support, and adoption.

Expert witness One, who by reason of education or specialized experience, possesses superior knowledge respecting a subject about which persons having no particular training are incapable of forming an accurate opinion or deducing correct conclusions. A witness who has been qualified as an expert, and who thereby will be allowed (through his or her answers to questions posted) to assist the court in understanding complicated and technical subjects not within the understanding of the average layperson.

Gault decision A landmark Supreme Court decision in 1967 that found that juveniles were entitled to the same due process rights as adults: the right to counsel, the right to notice of specific charges of the offense, the right to confront and cross-examine a witness, the right to remain silent, and the right to subpoena witnesses in defense. The right to trial by jury was not included. See Appendix 5.

Guardian ad litem An individual appointed by the court to represent the best interests of the child. This person may or may not be a lawyer.

Informed consent A person's agreement to allow something to happen (such as surgery) that is based on a full disclosure of facts needed to make the decision intelligently; i.e., disclosure of risks involved, alternatives, etc. Informed consent is the name for a general principle of law that a physician has a duty to disclose what a reasonably prudent physician, in the medical community, in the exercise of reasonable care, would disclose to his or her patient as to whatever grave risks of injury might be incurred from a proposed course of treatment, so that a patient, exercising ordinary care for his or her own welfare and faced with a choice of undergoing the proposed treatment, or alternative treatment, or none at all, may intelligently exercise judgment by reasonably balancing the probable risks against the probable benefits.

Insanity Not a clinical term, but a social and legal one, that indicates that the behavior of a person suffering from the condition is unreliable and thus likely to present a danger to himself or herself and others. The test for insanity differs from one jurisdiction to another, so it is important to determine what test is applicable in a given case.

> **American Law Institute, Model Penal Code** A person is not responsible for criminal conduct if at the time of such conduct as a result of mental disease or defect he or she lacks substantial capacity either to appreciate the criminality (wrongfulness) of his or her conduct or to conform his or her conduct to the requirements of the law.

> **Diminished Responsibility Doctrine (partial insanity)** Some jurisdictions permit the trier of fact to consider the impaired mental state of the accused in mitigation of the punishment or degree of the crime even though the impairment does not qualify as insanity.

> **Durham Rule** When there is some evidence that the accused suffered from a diseased or defective mental condition at the time the unlawful act was committed, he or she is not criminally responsible if it is found beyond a reasonable doubt that the act was the product of the mental abnormality.

M'Naughten Rule (used in the majority of jurisdictions) An accused is not criminally responsible if at the time of committing the criminal act, she or he was laboring under such a defect of reason from mental disease that the person did not know or understand the nature or quality of the act being committed, or was unable to distinguish right from wrong.

Juvenile Defined by state statute, but a youth under the age of 18 in a majority of states; a minor.

Juvenile court A court that has exclusive and original jurisdiction relative to juveniles as defined by state statute.

Juvenile delinquent A minor who has been adjudicated as having violated a federal, state, or local law. See *Delinquent child*.

Law guardian A term used in some states to refer to a public defender.

Neglected child A child is "neglected" when his or her parent or custodian, by reason of cruelty, mental incapacity, immorality, or depravity, is unfit to properly care for him or her, or neglects or refuses to provide necessary physical, affectional, medical, surgical, or institutional or hospital care; or the child is in such condition of want or suffering, or is under such improper care or control as to endanger his or her morals or health.

PINS Person in need of supervision. See *status offender*.

Petition A statement of a cause of action against an alleged offender. The petition must state with specificity the act complained of and a violation of either federal, state, or municipal statute or ordinance wherein the violation lies.

Privacy, right of The right to be left alone; the right of a person to be free from unwarranted publicity.

Privileged communications Those statements made by certain persons within a protected relationship such as husband-wife, attorney-client, priest-penitent, therapist-patient, and the like which the law protects from forced disclosure on the witness stand. The extent of the privilege is governed by state or federal statutes.

Probable cause Reasonable cause; having more evidence for than against. A reasonable ground for belief in the existence of facts warranting the proceedings complained of. An apparent state of facts found to exist upon reasonable inquiry (i.e., such inquiry as the given case renders convenient and proper) that would induce a reasonably intelligent and prudent man to believe, in a criminal case, that the accused person had committed the crime charged or, in a civil case, that a cause of action existed.

Standards of proof The burden of proof required to prevail in a particular type of case. In a criminal case, the prosecutor has the burden of proving his or her case beyond a reasonable doubt. In most civil cases, the plaintiff must prove his or her case by a preponderance of evidence. In juvenile and certain other proceedings, the prosecution must prove its case by clear and convincing evidence, variously defined but usually to mean more than a preponderance but not beyond a reasonable doubt.

Status offender (PINS, CHINS, unruly child) A minor who has committed an act that is not a crime if committed by an adult but is considered illegal by the laws of the state. Though some variations exist from state to state, the behavior that is usually encompassed by the term includes truancy, running away from home, and ungovernability (being beyond reasonable control of one's parents).

Termination of parental rights A clear and convincing finding that the parents have either failed to provide the proper care for a child, have abandoned the child, have physically or sexually abused the child, and have failed to cooperate under a proposed case plan designed to reunify the parents and child. If a court, after trial, determines that the parents will not be able to provide the proper care and support in the foreseeable future for the child, the court may terminate parental rights and grant permanent custody to either a relative or to an appropriate state department that may assume custody for purposes of adoptive placement.

Training school An institution operated by the state to rehabilitate the juvenile offender. Usually the equivalent of a correctional school or institution.

Transfer or transfer hearing See *waiver*.

Unruly child See *status offender*.

Waiver The act by which a juvenile court transfers a juvenile to an adult court for criminal prosecution.

Definitions are from *Black's Law Dictionary* (St. Paul, MN, West, 1989. Used with permission); *A Psychiatric Dictionary*, 6th Edition, edited by R. J. Campbell, M.D. (New York, Oxford University Press, 1989); Judge W. Don Reader; Helen Sacks, M.S.W.; and Sandra Nye, J.D.

BIBLIOGRAPHY

A rising tide of violence leaves more youths in jail. The New York Times, July 2, 1990, p 4

Aber MS, Repucci ND: The limits of mental health expertise in juvenile and family law. Int J Law Psychiatry 10:167–185, 1987

American Academy of Child Psychiatry: Child Psychiatry: A Plan for the Coming Decades. Washington, DC, American Academy of Child Psychiatry, 1983

American Bar Association: Juvenile Justice Standards: Summary and Analysis. Cambridge, MA, Ballinger Press, 1977

American Bar Association and the Institute of Judicial Administration: Juvenile Justice Standards Relating to Transfer Between Courts. Cambridge, MA, Ballinger Press, 1980

American Medical Association: Common Health Problems of Juveniles in Correctional Facilities. Chicago, IL, American Medical Association, 1979

American Medical Association Council on Scientific Affairs: Health status of detained and incarcerated youth. JAMA 263:987–991, 1990

American Psychiatric Association: Clinical Aspects of the Violent Individual (Task Force Report No 8). Washington, DC, American Psychiatric Association, 1974

American Psychiatric Association: Response to Juvenile Justice Standards Project of the ABA/IJA. Washington, DC, American Psychiatric Association, 1978

Bailey G: Current perspectives on substance abuse in youth. J Am Acad Child Adolesc Psychiatry 28(2):151–162, 1989

Bank SC, Poythress NG Jr: The elements of persuasion in expert testimony. Journal of Psychiatry and the Law 10(2):173–204, 1982

Barnum R: Integrating multiple perspectives in forensic child psychiatry consultation. J Am Acad Child Psychiatry 25(5):718–723, 1986

Barnum R: Clinical evaluation of juvenile delinquents facing transfer to adult court. J Am Acad Child Adolesc Psychiatry 26(6):922–925, 1987

Becker JV, Kavoussi RJ: Diagnosis and treatment of juvenile sex offenders, in Juvenile Psychiatry and the Law. Edited by Rosner R, Schwartz HI. New York, Plenum, 1989, pp 133–143

Benedek EP: Forensic training for child psychiatrists. Bull Am Acad Psychiatry Law 2(4):262–265, 1974

Benedek EP: Psychiatry and juvenile law. Psychiatr Clin North Am 6(4):695–705, 1983

Benedek EP: Forensic child psychiatry training. Paper presented at the annual meeting of the American Academy of Child Psychiatry, 1984

Benedek EP: Waiver of juveniles to adult court, in Emerging Issues in Child Psychiatry and the Law. Edited by Schetky DH, Benedek EP. New York, Brunner/Mazel, 1985, pp 180–190

Benedek EP: Forensic child psychiatry: an emerging subspecialty. Bull Am Acad Psychiatry Law 14:295–300, 1986

Benedek EP: Capital crimes and capital punishment in minors. Paper presented at the annual meeting of the American Psychiatric Association. New York, May 1990

Benedek EP, Cornell DG: Juvenile Homicide. Washington, DC, American Psychiatric Press, 1989

Blos P: The second individuation process of adolescence. Psychoanal Study Child 22:162–186, 1967

Boat B, Everson M: Using Anatomical Dolls: Guidelines for Interviewing Young Children in Sexual Abuse Investigations. Chapel Hill, NC, University of North Carolina, 1986

Burnstein MH: Court-ordered psychiatric evaluation of juveniles. Hosp Community Psychiatry 38(1):77–78, 1987

Chatterjee SK: Drugs and the young: some legal issues. Bull Narc 37 (2–3):157–168, 1985

Child Abuse Prevention Act (1974), 42 USCSS 5101-5106 et seq (1982) (as amended)

Cornell DG, Hawk EL: Clinical presentation of malingerers diagnosed by experienced forensic examiners. Law and Human Behavior 13:375–383, 1989

Cornell DG, Benedek EP, Benedek DM: Juvenile homicide: prior adjustment and a proposed typology. Am J Orthopsychiatry 57(3):383–393, 1987

Cox FN: Psychological test evidence in the criminal courts: a case study. Med Law 3(2):163–170, 1984

Davis GE, Leitenberg H: Adolescent sex offenders. Psychol Bull 101:417–427, 1987

DeLeon G: Legal pressure in therapeutic communities. NIDA Research Monograph 86:160–177, 1988

Drukteinis AM: Criminal responsibility of juvenile offenders. American Journal of Forensic Psychology 4(2):33–48, 1986

Dusky v United States, 362 US 402, 1960

Eth S: Adolescent separation-individuation and the court. Bull Am Acad Psychiatry Law 11(3):231–238, 1983

Eth S, Schowalter JE: Resolved: there is no special developmental consideration in adolescence mitigating against capital punishment for those who committed murder under eighteen years of age. J Am Acad Child Adolesc Psychiatry 28(3):450–454, 1989

Ex Parte Crouse, 1838

Federal Rules of Evidence 7

Fialkov MJ: Fostering permanency of children in out-of-home care: psychological aspects. Bull Am Acad Psychiatry Law 16:343–357, 1988

Friedman V, Morgan M: Interviewing Sexual Abuse Victims Using Anatomical Dolls: The Professional's Guidebook. Eugene, OR, Shamrock Press, 1985

Gardner MR: Punitive juvenile justice: some observations on a recent trend. Int J Law Psychiatry 10:129–151, 1987

Gardner RA: Family Evaluation in Child Custody Litigation. Cresskill, NJ, Creative Therapy, 1982

Giallombardo R (ed): Juvenile Delinquency, A Book of Readings, 2nd Edition. New York, John Wiley, 1972

Gleaton T, Gowen S: The adolescent drug epidemic and the chronic young adult patient: is there a link? Fair Oaks Hospital Psychiatry Letter [Summit, NJ] 3(2), 1985

Glueck S, Glueck E: Unraveling Juvenile Delinquency. New York, Commonwealth Fund, 1950

Goetz JD: Children's rights under the Burger Court: concern for the child but deference to authority. Notre Dame Law Review 5:1214–1232, 1985

Goldstein J, Freud A, Solnit A, et al: In the Best Interests of the Child. New York, Free Press, 1986

Goldzband MG, Schetky DH: Should adult psychiatrists be doing child custody evaluations? Bull Am Acad Psychiatry Law 14:361–366, 1986

Grisso T: Juveniles' Waiver of Rights: Legal and Psychological Competence. New York, Plenum, 1981

Grisso T, Miller MO, Sales B: Competency to stand trial in juvenile court. Int J Law Psychiatry 10:1–20, 1987

Groth AN: The adolescent sexual offender and his prey. International Journal of Offender Therapy and Comparative Criminology 21:249–254, 1977

Groth AN, Loredo CM: Juvenile sex offenders: guidelines for assessment. International Journal of Offender Therapy and Comparative Criminology 25:31–39, 1981

Hamparian DM, Estep LK, Muntean SM, et al: Youth in Adult Court: Between Two Worlds. Columbus, OH, Academy for Contemporary Problems, 1982

Harrington MM, Keary AO: The insanity defense in juvenile delinquency proceedings. Bull Am Acad Psychiatry Law 8(3):272–279, 1980

Hathaway SR, McKinley JC: Minnesota Multiphasic Personality Inventory—2. Minneapolis, University of Minnesota, 1989

Helfer RE, Kempe CH: The Battered Child. Chicago, IL, University of Chicago Press, 1987, pp 152–177

Iacono WG, Patrick CJ: Assessing deception: polygraph techniques, in Clinical Assessment of Malingering and Deception. Edited by Rogers R. New York, Guilford, 1988, pp 205–234

In re Gault, 387 US 1, 1967

In re Winship, 397 US 358, 1970

Institute of Judicial Administration, American Bar Association: Standards for Juvenile Justice: Summary and Analysis, 2nd Edition. Cambridge, MA, Ballinger Press, 1982

Jackson v Indiana, 406 US 715, 92 SCt 1845, 32 L.Ed.2d 435, 1972

Jesness CA: The Jesness Inventory Manual. Palo Alto, CA, Consulting Psychologists Press, 1983

Johnson AM, Szurek SA: The genesis of antisocial acting out in children and adults. Psychoanal Q 21:323–332, 1952

Juvenile Justice Delinquency Prevention Act of 1974, 88 Stat 1109

Kalogerakis MG: The sources of individual violence, in Adolescent Psychiatry, Vol 3. Edited by Feinstein SC, Giovacchini PL. Chicago, IL, University of Chicago Press, 1974, pp 323–339

Kempe CH, Silverman FN, Steele BF, et al: The battered-child syndrome. JAMA 181:17–24, 1962

Kent v United States, 383 US 541, 1966

Levine M, Ewing CP, Hager R: Juvenile and family mental health law in sociohistorical context. Int J Law Psychiatry 10:91–109, 1987

Levine RS: Disaffirmance of the right to treatment doctrine: a new juncture in juvenile justice. University of Pittsburgh Law Review 2:159–204, 1980

Lewis DO: Diagnostic evaluation of the delinquent child: psychiatric, psychological, neurological, and educational components, in Child Psychiatry and the Law. Edited by Schetky DH, Benedek EP. New York, Brunner/Mazel, 1980, pp 139–155

Lewis DO, Shanok SS, Pincus JH: Violent juvenile delinquents: psychiatric, neurological, psychological and base factors. J Am Acad Child Psychiatry 18:307–318, 1979

Marohn R: Hospital treatment of the behaviorally disordered adolescent, in The Treatment of Antisocial Syndromes. Edited by Reid W. New York, Van Nostrand Reinhold, 1981, pp 146–161

Malmquist CP: Children who witness violence, tortious aspects. Bull Am Acad Psychiatry Law 13(3):221–231, 1985

Mathew v Nelson, 461 FSupp 707, 1978

McDermott JF Jr: Certification of the child psychiatrist. J Am Acad Child Psychiatry 14(2):196–203, 1975

McKeiver v Pennsylvania, 403 US 528, 1971

Melton GB: Law and random events: the state of child mental health policy. Int J Law Psychiatry 10:81–90, 1987

Melton GB, Petrila J, Poythress NG, et al: Psychological Evaluations for the Courts. New York, Guilford, 1987

Millon T, Green CJ, Meagher RB Jr: Millon Adolescent Personality Inventory. Minneapolis, MN, NCS Interpretive Scoring System, 1976–82

Monahan J: The Clinical Prediction of Violent Behavior. Rockville, MD, U.S. Department of Health and Human Services, 1981

Morrison HL: The forensic evaluation and treatment of children: ethics and values. Bull Am Acad Psychiatry Law 14(4):353–359, 1986

Morse SJ, Whitebread CH: Mental health implications of the juvenile justice standards. Child and Youth Services 5(1–2):5–27, 1982

Mulvey EP, Repucci ND: Perceptions of appropriate services for juvenile offenders. Criminal Justice and Behavior 11(4):401–422, 1984

Murray CA, Cox LA: Beyond Probation. Beverly Hills, CA, Sage, 1979

National Adolescent Perpetrator Network: Preliminary report from the national Task Force in Juvenile Sexual Offending. Juvenile and Family Court Journal 39:5–52, 1988

National Advisory Committee for Juvenile Justice and Delinquency Prevention: Serious Juvenile Crime: A Redirected Federal Effort. Washington, DC, U.S. Department of Justice, Office of Juvenile Justice and Delinquency Prevention, 1984

National Institute on Drug Abuse: National Household Survey on Drug Abuse. Washington, DC, U.S. Department of Health and Human Services, 1989

Peterson H, Millman R: Substance abuse among juveniles, in Juvenile Psychiatry and the Law. Edited by Rosner R, Schwartz H. New York, Plenum, 1989, pp 237–256

Platt AM: The Child Savers, The Invention of Juvenile Delinquency. Chicago, IL, University of Chicago Press, 1969

Quinn KM: Competency to be a witness: a major child forensic issue. Bull Am Acad Psychiatry Law 14(4):311–321, 1986

Quinn KM: The credibility of children's allegations of sexual abuse. Behavioral Sciences and the Law 6:181–200, 1988

Ratner R: Biological causes of delinquency, in Juvenile Psychiatry and the Law. Edited by Rosner R, Schwartz H. New York, Plenum, 1989, pp 29–44

Rosenbaum M: Just Say What? An Alternative View on Solving America's Drug Problem. San Francisco, CA, National Council on Crime & Delinquency, 1989

Rosner R, Schwartz H (eds): Juvenile Psychiatry and the Law. New York, Plenum, 1989

Rutter M, Giller H: Juvenile Delinquency. New York, Guilford, 1984

Santosky v Kramer, 50 USLW 4333 (US, March 24, 1982)

Savitsky JC, Karras D: Competency to stand trial among adolescents. Adolescence 19(Summer):349–358, 1984

Schall v Martin, 467 US 253, 1984

Schetky DH, Benedek EP (eds): Child Psychiatry and the Law. New York, Brunner/Mazel, 1980

Schetky D, Benedek EP (eds): Emerging Issues in Child Psychiatry and the Law. New York, Brunner/Mazel, 1985

Schetky D, Angell R, Morrison CV, et al: "Parents who fail," a study of 51 cases of termination of parental rights. J Am Acad Child Adolesc Psychiatry 18:366–383, 1979

Schoettle UC: Termination of parental rights—ethical issues and role conflicts. J Am Acad Child Adolesc Psychiatry 23:629–632, 1984

Sgroi SM (ed): Handbook of Clinical Intervention in Child Sexual Abuse. Lexington, MA, Heath, 1982

Shanok SS, Lewis DO: Juvenile court versus child guidance referral: psychosocial and parental factors. Am J Psychiatry 134(10):1130–1133, 1977

Shepherd RD: Transfer or waiver of jurisdiction. Criminal Justice 3(2):28, 1988

Shuman DW: The diagnostic and statistical manual of mental disorders in the courts. Bull Am Acad Psychiatry Law 17(1):25–32, 1989

Skaste D: Child Custody Evaluation: A Practical Guide. Beverly Hills, CA, Sage, 1985

Slovenko R: Psychiatry and the Law. Boston, MA, Little, Brown, 1973

Stanford v Kentucky, 87-5765, 1989

State of Oregon Children's Services: Oregon Report on Juvenile Sex Offenders. Portland, OR, 1986

Stewart D, Gangbar R: Psychiatric assessment of competency to care for a newborn. Can J Psychiatry 29:583–589, 1984

Stone AA: Overview: the right to treatment—comments on the law and its impact. Am J Psychiatry 132:1125–1134, 1975

Task Force on Juvenile Justice Issues: The psychiatrist and the juvenile justice system. Am J Psychiatry 174:1584–1586, 1990

Thompson v Oklahoma, 101 L.Ed.2nd 702, 1988

Travin S, Cullen K, Melella JT: The use and abuse of erection measurements: a forensic perspective. Bull Am Acad Psychiatry Law 16:235–250, 1988

U.S. Department of Justice: Juvenile Court Statistics, 1984. Washington, DC, Office of Juvenile Justice and Delinquency Prevention, 1987

Wechsler D: Wechsler Intelligence Scale for Children, Revised. San Antonio, TX, Psychological Corporation, 1974

Weithorn LA (ed): Psychology and Child Custody Determination: Knowledge, Roles and Expertise. Lincoln, University of Nebraska Press, 1987

White S, Quinn KM: Investigatory independence in child sexual abuse evaluations: conceptual considerations. Bull Am Acad Psychiatry Law 16:269–273, 1988

White S, Strom G, Santilli G, et al: Clinical guidelines for interviewing young children with anatomically correct dolls (unpublished manuscript). Cleveland, OH, Case Western Reserve University School of Medicine, 1987

Whitebread CH, Heilman J: An overview of the law of juvenile delinquency. Behavioral Sciences and the Law 6(3):285–305, 1988

Wilkins v Missouri, 87-6026, 1989

INDEX

Abuse. *See* Physical abuse; Sexual abuse; Substance abuse
Adjudication
  competency assessment, 27–30
  description, 14
  transfer or waiver to adult court, 31, 33
Adoption Assistance and Child Welfare Act of 1980, 122
Adversary witnesses, 61
Alcoholics Anonymous, 16
American Academy of Child and Adolescent Psychiatry, 126
American Bar Association, 9
American Law Institute Model Penal Code, 32
American Psychiatric Association, 9
  position on dangerousness, 75
Arraignment, 14, 26
Attachment behavior, 43, 94–95

Bailiffs, 22
Big Brothers, 16
Big Sisters, 16
Burden of proof
  in judicial transfer, 81
  sexual abuse cases, 97
  termination of parental rights, 122

Case examples
  abuse and neglect evaluations, 42, 43
  applying psychiatric thinking to legal questions, 56

attachment behavior, 94–95
competency, 29, 45
delinquency and status offense evaluations, 39, 40, 41
expert witness standards, 62–63
hearsay evidence, 67
insanity defense, 32
intake phase, 26–27
psychiatric recommendation samples, 145–147
sexual abuse, 98, 99–100, 103
termination of parental rights, 122–123
transfer or waiver to adult court, 31
Child Abuse Prevention Act, 93
"Child savers" movement, 6
Child sexual abuse. *See* Sexual abuse
Clinical evaluations
  abuse and neglect cases, 42–44, 75
  antisocial activities history, 40
  assumption of veracity, 37–38
  attachment behaviors, 43
  competency, 44–45
  court-ordered, 133–134
  data to support conclusions, 43
  delinquency and status offense evaluations, 39–42
  denial, 38–39
  family assessment, 43
  family history, 40
  format, 38
  free play, 101
  impact, 37
  informed consent, 134, 159–161